X/20

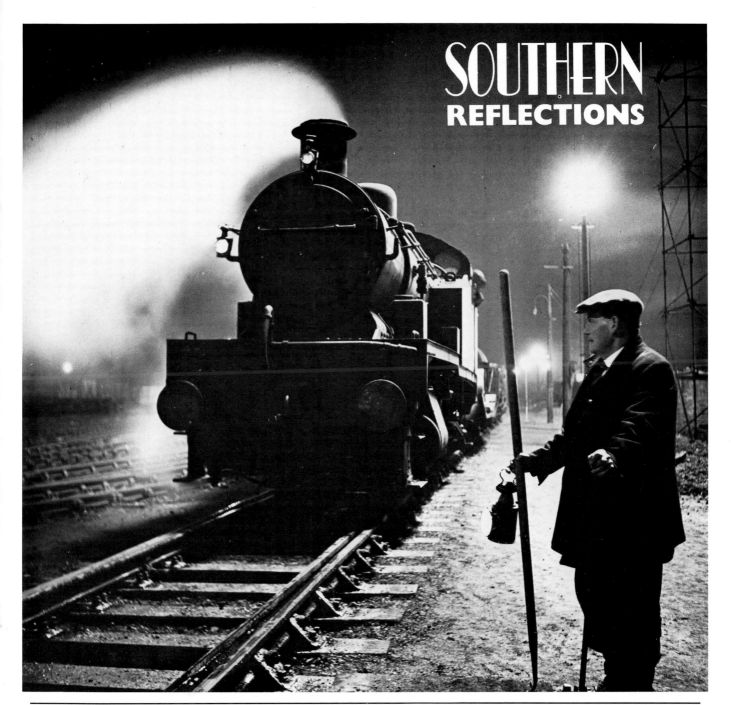

SOUTHERN REFLECTIONS

A COLLECTION OF PHOTOGRAPHS FROM THE BBC HULTON PICTURE LIBRARY

by

R.C. RILEY & NIGEL HARRIS

Silver Link Publishing Ltd

THE COACH HOUSE, GARSTANG ROAD, ST MICHAEL'S ON WYRE, LANCASHIRE, PR3 0TG

CONTENTS

ACKNOWLEDGEMENTS

THE photographs in this book were produced mainly as news or feature photographs for contemporary publications, with the exception of those commissioned by the LSWR, which often used the Topical Press Agency to take photographs for use in the *South Western Gazette* and other railway journals. The captions surviving in the TPA files were either of a very general nature, or in the case of the LSWR pictures, merely listed under subject headings. In some cases, expert advice was sought and grateful thanks are due in respect of certain subjects to: Phil Atkins, Librarian, National Railway Museum,

York (Accident reports); Denis Cullum (Signalling); Derek Winkworth (Imperial Airways); Michael Ware, Curator, National Motor Museum (Earl Howe's car) and finally, Geoff Lumb and Bill Thornycroft (Railway owned road vehicles). It should be emphasised that none of these gentlemen have seen the finished manuscript and the compilers must accept responsibility for any errors of interpretation.

In closing, I would like to express my gratitude to my wife Christine and my sons David and Philip for their support during compilation of this book. ***RCR, April 1988.***

PUBLISHER'S ACKNOWLEDGEMENTS

THIS book concludes the quartet of 'Reflections' volumes produced by SLP in association with the BBC Hulton Picture Library, and the publishers would like to thank Dick Riley for a first-rate job in researching the text and captions to the pictures which appear in these pages. The publishers would also like to record their thanks and appreciation to everyone at the BBC who has become involved with this series for their enthusiastic assistance. Selecting the pictures for the four volumes and the collating of negatives for printing was a

marathon task and we are most grateful for the help we received. Special thanks are due to Janet Andrew, Head of BBC Data Services & Sales, BBC Hulton Picture Library Acting Manager Bob Bright, HPL Deputy Manager Roger Wemyss-Brooks and BBC Data Marketing Manager Peter Elliott. Finally, many thanks indeed to Tristram Elliott, Assistant in Charge, Negative Unit and Picture Researcher Louisa Upton, who devoted much time and effort in the task of sifting out negatives and original captions for this book. ***NH, April 1988.***

Southern Reflections: a collection of photographs from the BBC Hulton Picture Library.
1. Southern. England. Railway Services.
British Rail Southern Region - Illustration.
1 Riley, R.C. (Richard Callcott)
2. Harris Nigel
385'.09422
ISBN 0 947971 22 X

Left: Pride and determination - a quite superb portrait of an engineman. This picture of an unnamed driver was taken in August 1944 by *Picture Post* photographer Heywood Magee. The driver is clearly proud of his role: he is wearing a neat collar and tie, whilst prominent on his waistcoat are medal ribbons, doubtless earned during the First World War. Also, note the carefully waxed moustache! The occasion was the running by the SR of a special train, hauled by Maunsell 'King Arthur' 4-6-0 No. 788 *Sir Urre of the Mount*, for American soldiers, from Clapham Junction to Southampton.

Front cover: No. 21C1 *Channel Packet* stands at Victoria on April 12 1946 at the head of the inaugural post-war down 'Golden Arrow.' Departure was at 10.00am, the run to Dover being allowed 1hr 40min, with eventual arrival in Paris at 6.45pm. As conditions improved, these times were accelerated; even so, the pre-war timings were never achieved again. Much more fuss was made of this train in post-war days: the train was provided with a headboard, clean flags daily, while the regular engines had to be drilled with special holes to take the long arrow emblem carried on each side of the boiler. Until closure of Stewarts Lane in 1961, the engines rostered to this duty were always in beautiful condition. The train was electrically hauled until withdrawal in 1972.

Previous Page: An evocative after-dark picture at Hither Green yard in February 1948, with a 'Z' class 0-8-0T on duty.

Rear Cover: Pioneer Bulleid 'Pacific' No. 21C1 *Channel Packet*, at Alresford on March 10 1941, with a VIPs train, following official naming at Eastleigh. See also pages 92-95.

THE Southern Railway grew from wonderfully diverse beginnings, starting in 1830 with the line from Canterbury to Whitstable Harbour. Long rivalry in the south east caused considerable duplication of lines by the South Eastern and the London Chatham & Dover Railways (which soon gained the nickname the London Smashem and Turnover Railway) but their obvious joint management as the South Eastern & Chatham Railway did not come about until 1900. The west was occupied by the London & South Western Railway (very much intermingled with the Great Western Railway), linking London with Portsmouth and Plymouth. Sandwiched between these companies was the London Brighton & South Coast Railway, whose sharing of Victoria station with the SECR could cause confusion. Many notable engineers developed steam traction for these early companies. The LSWR had Adams and Drummond, whose 'M7' 0-4-4Ts outlived the Southern Railway. The LBSCR had Stroudley (whose 'Terrier' 0-6-0Ts have been going strong since 1872) and Marsh, who scored by having Kitson build him some Ivatt-like 'Atlantics.' Incidentally, Ivatt retired to Haywards Heath in 1911 and enjoyed seeing them sprinting past, albeit under the disguise of LBSCR cabs and chimneys. Maunsell of the SECR took over as CME of the SR in 1923 and his notable designs included the 'Schools' 4-4-0 and 'Lord Nelson' 4-6-0s.

The present Waterloo station was completed in 1922. It replaced a chaotic assembly of ad hoc extensions well described in Chapter V of *Three Men in a Boat*, by Jerome K. Jerome. All the other London termini, except London Bridge, were across the River Thames, and there was even a station at The Bank, on the City 'tube' line, of 1898. Many SR lines radiate from London, but there is also a line from Guildford to Ashford and on to Folkestone and Dover. They were all in the front line during two World Wars.

For many years, even minor stations had busy goods sidings but as more and more lorries appeared for local haulage these began to fall into disuse, and many became moribund. This factor, combined with declining goods traffic in the early 1930s, caused problems for the other three main line companies, but the SR was hit less hard, owing to its intensive passenger traffic extending electrification and ports traffic.

Despite its optimistic outlook, the SR had started life hampered by a decidedly comic image. I remember it well; it probably had its roots in the early clashes between its constituents and was fuelled by the gruesomely slow and late trains of obsolete carriages on the suburban lines. Herbert Walker, General Manager of the LSWR since 1912, became first General Manager of the SR and by 1925 had installed John Elliot to improve its public image. This was a notable success, despite some head-shaking when, for example, he allowed a film company to wreck a train at Lasham, on the soon to be closed Basingstoke-Alton line, in 1928 for *The Wrecker*.

Many practical improvements by Herbert Walker had made the SR the envy of the northern companies by 1937, but the company's steam fleet was in decline and to remedy this my father was appointed as Chief Mechanical Engineer, to succeed Maunsell, who was due to retire. The war overshadowed the impact of the early Bulleid locomotives and incidentally, the SR workshops at Ashford, Brighton and Eastleigh all performed a noble share of special war work, in addition to their normal duties. Very soon after, the dramatic war exploits by the 'Pacifics' were making headlines and they also scored maximum points for sustained power during the 1948 locomotive exchanges. My father was very pleased by the praise they earned from drivers and firemen.

For every passenger who is enthusiastic about the locomotive at the head of the train there must be a dozen or more who simply want a comfortable and punctual journey. The

FOREWORD
by
H.A.V.BULLEID
MA, FI Mech E, ARPS

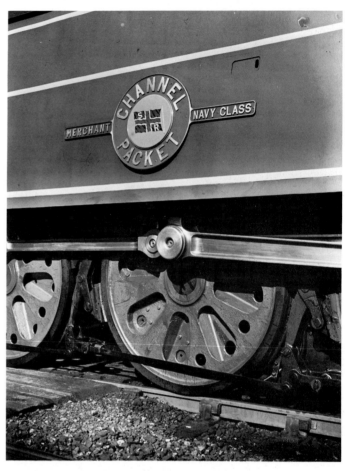

Above: On March 10 1941, the nameplate of pioneer Bulleid 'Merchant Navy' 4-6-2 No. 21C1 *Channel Packet* is pictured whilst the engine paused at Alresford, for its VIP passengers to enjoy lunch following the naming ceremony at Eastleigh. Bulleid 'Pacifics' are still common at Alresford, for the Mid Hants Railway cares for working examples of 'West Country' 4-6-2s in both original and rebuilt forms, and an unrestored (at the time of going to press) 'Merchant Navy.'

'Pacifics' certainly added punctuality, and most Bulleid carriages rode better and provided rather more space than their predecessors. For commuters weary of standing, the two double deck EMU trains added greater capacity, compared with standard stock. Writers regularly describe my father's 0-6-0 and his 12-wheeled tank engine, but Southern steam is best remembered with his 'Pacifics.' A few appear in this book and 31 examples are preserved, with an increasing number returning to steam as the years pass.

H.A.V. Bulleid

Chapter 1: Constituent Companies
THE LONDON & SOUTH WESTERN RAILWAY

THE London & South Western Railway started life on July 25 1834 as the London & Southampton Railway, whose London terminus was located at Nine Elms, site of the present day fruit and vegetable market, formerly based at Covent Garden. The first section of line, from Nine Elms to Woking Common (23 miles) opened on May 19 1838, with the next section to Shapley Heath (Winchfield) opening on September 24. On June 4 1839, the Company changed its name by Act of Parliament to the London & South Western Railway, in readiness for the opening of the final section of line to Southampton, on June 10, The LSWR's route linked the capital to Southampton via Wimbledon, Esher, Walton, Weybridge, Woking, Farnborough, Basingstoke, Micheldever and Winchester. The elegant Southampton terminus, designed by William Tite, was closed to passenger traffic in 1966, since when the building has been expertly restored and is now in use as a casino!

The LSWR served Portsmouth indirectly from 1841, via a branch from Bishopstoke (now Eastleigh) to Gosport, passengers thence proceeding by ferry to their destination. Gosport station was also built to William Tite's design, but it sustained damage during enemy action in 1941 and after closure to passengers in 1955, and subsequent withdrawal of freight facilities, this once-fine building has been allowed to decay. Perhaps some entrepreneur might like to appeal to the gambling instinct in Gosport and provide a future!

Nine Elms station was abandoned

Below: The London & Southampton Railway (later LSWR) terminus at Nine Elms, on January 19 1951, when it was contemplated that this building should be the home of a railway museum; nothing came of the suggestion. The original Topical Press caption reads: "A permanent transport museum housed in Nine Elms station.......is proposed by a committee representing all the State transport executives. The British Transport Commission has accepted the committee's recommendations in principle, and, as suggested, will appoint a small staff for the expert supervision of the various relics which passed to the Commission with the integration of the main line railway companies, and the London Passenger Transport Board. The Committee suggested Nine Elms station as a comprehensive museum because they wished to secure a building of historical railway interest, the terminus here being a building of architectural distinction, erected in 1838 to the design of Sir William Tite, architect of the Royal Exchange."

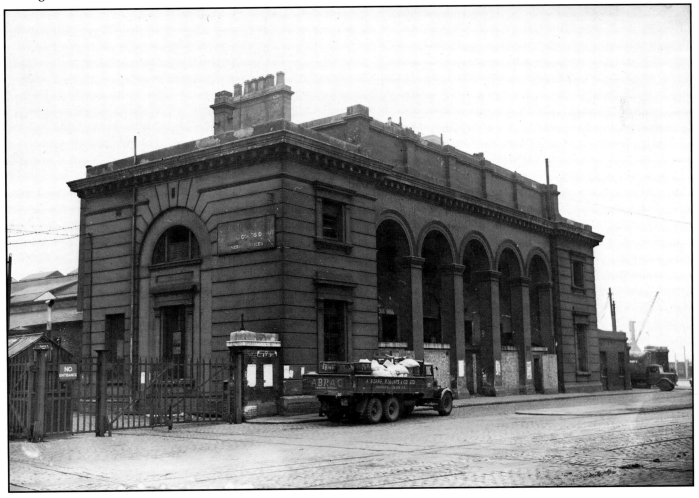

(other than for goods traffic) when Waterloo opened for business in 1848. By this time, the LSWR had also reached Dorchester, by way of a circuitous route via Wimborne and Poole (for Bournemouth still awaited development at that time) and also Salisbury. The LSWR clearly entertained ambitions in the West Country, for in 1845 the Company had acquired the impecunious Bodmin & Wadebridge Company, dating from 1834. Even so, the LSWR was not physically connected to the BWR branch until 1895 (when the Halwill-Wadebridge link was completed) and in its advance to the West the LSWR had to obtain running powers over the metals of the less-than-enthusiastic GWR, at both Exeter and Plymouth. Curiously, as a result of geographical 'quirks' at both locations, LSWR trains ran in opposite directions to their GWR counterparts; thus the LSWR's 'down' trains at both Exeter and Plymouth ran over the GWR's 'up' line, and vice versa!

Nearer to London, the LSWR steadily consolidated its important presence by building an impressive outer suburban network, and by degrees gradually encompassed much of Hampshire and Dorset, and also parts of Wiltshire, Devon and Cornwall. The Company eventually covered an extensive area of coastline, from Southsea to Exmouth, and from Padstow to Ilfracombe.

Within such a large area, the LSWR's principal passenger services covered long distances and from the turn of the century its passenger coaches provided a good standard of travel. Unlike the other two principal Southern Railway constituents (the London Brighton & South Coast Railway and the South Eastern & Chatham Railways, which used Pullman Cars) the LSWR appreciated the need both for corridor coaches and also dining saloons, of which it owned 29 examples by 1922. The LSWR also employed highly capable locomotive engineers, including J. and W.G. Beattie, William Adams, Dugald Drummond and Robert Urie. Adams was noted for his 'Highflyer' 4-4-0s, and whilst Drummond also designed and built some excellent 4-4-0s, his 4-6-0s were less than successful. Robert Urie built thoroughly solid, reliable and strong engines, with some designs being perpetuated after the Grouping of 1923.

With the appointment of Herbert Walker as General Manager in 1912 (who subsequently held the position with the Southern Railway, until 1937) the LSWR was fortunate to have a thoroughly forward-looking man in charge. Indeed, he has been described in some circles as the greatest railway General Manager of the 20th century. He initiated the extension of Southampton Docks (acquired by the LSWR in 1892) and carried out the electrification of the inner suburban lines, which doubled their traffic between 1913 and 1920. By 1922, the LSWR under Walker's stewardship owned 873 route miles of track, 931 locomotives, 4,061 passenger vehicles and 14,563 goods vehicles. During 1921 the Company's trains had conveyed 65 million passengers, making the LSWR the largest partner in the SR, which came into being in 1923.

By the turn of the century, the LSWR's thoughts had turned to quadrupling its main line beyond Basingstoke, to Worting Junction (51 miles from Waterloo) where the Bournemouth and Salisbury/Exeter lines diverged. Battledown Flyover, which eliminated the need for conflicting movements at this junction, was brought into use in 1897, at the same time as the line from Basingtoke was being quadrupled. By autumn 1904, the line from Clapham Junction to Basingstoke was quadrupled, and in order to serve four tracks, Basingstoke station was rebuilt. It was claimed in 1905 that the Stationmaster's large staff of 130 included: 14 clerks, 21 shunters, 22 signalmen, 14 porters, 18 Inspectors, Foremen, Guards and Ticket Collectors, and 41 staff whose duties were described as 'miscellaneous.' This very large complement of staff was needed to handle Basingstoke's hectic traffic, which at this time featured 226 passenger and freight trains daily.

BASINGSTOKE

Above: Looking east from Basingstoke in 1917, showing the crossover to the GWR line to Reading, also used by LSWR trains. Behind the railings to the left is the independent GWR terminus, while beyond the the GWR clerestory coaches in the siding can be seen the GWR engine shed. The LSWR's engine shed was located on the up side of the main line at the west end of the station. At this time, the LSWR's signalling was pneumatic, hence the interesting array of air pipes on the signal gantry, rather than the more usual network of pulleys and wires. Detail of interest to the railway modeller includes the small ground signals adjacent to the barrow crossing, also the station and yard lamp posts.

MOTIVE POWER

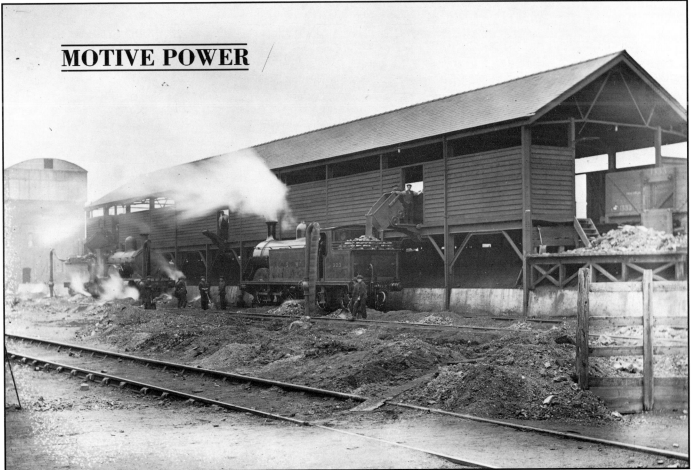

Above: An impressive view of the coaling stage and enormous water tower, at Eastleigh running sheds, one of the largest motive power depots on the LSWR system. It opened in 1903, replacing Northam shed, which was nearer Southampton. The LSWR Locomotive Works was originally at Nine Elms, but this site had limited scope for expansion and the Company therefore decided to build a new works at Eastleigh, hence the major importance of the neighbouring engine shed. The Carriage & Wagon Works had already been moved to Eastleigh, in 1891. As construction at Eastleigh progressed, men and equipment were gradually transferred to the new works, which eventually opened in 1910, no new locomotives having been built at Nine Elms since 1908. The engine pictured here alongside the coaling stage is one of Drummond's very successful Class M7 0-4-4Ts, No. 323, built at Nine Elms in 1900. The locomotive on the left, taking water from a column, is one of Adam's 'Highflyer' 4-4-0s, so-called because of their 'high-stepping' 7ft 1in diameter driving wheels. The coaling stage consists of a steel-framed building, with timber cladding. Coal was delivered in wooden-bodied wagons and shovelled manually into small steel tubs, as seen above No. 323's bunker.

Below: ' M7' 0-4-4T No. 38 (built 1898) is coaled by a small hoist in the locomotive sidings outside Waterloo station in March 1921. Coal was supplied to the LSWR in the private wagons of Stephenson Clarke & Co., London, who retained the fuel contract with the SR after the Grouping. The large building behind the crane was one of the electrical sub-stations which provided current for the suburban electric multiple unit services, the main generating station being located at Wimbledon. No. 38 was one of a batch of ten M7s built by the LSWR between March and June 1898, the engines costing £1,500 each to construct. Used for suburban passenger duties, the class served LSWR, SR and BR regimes - indeed, all bar one of the class of 105 engines survived to take BR numbers in 1948, although No. 672, had a very short career with the nationalised system: it fell down the Waterloo & City Line lift shaft at Waterloo and was broken up where it lay, wheels uppermost, on June 9 1948! Withdrawal commenced in 1957 and the 'M7s' were extinct by mid-1964.

Right: Another view of 'M7' No. 38, on the turntable in the Waterloo engine sidings, with the water tower visible on the right. Also visible in the right background is part of the building of the London Necropolis Company, which had its own private platform at Waterloo, for handling funeral trains worked by the LSWR over its line to Brookwood, where burials were carried out at the neighbouring cemetery. The irascible Dugald Drummond, designer of the 'M7', was interred there himself in 1911. Of the total of 105 'M7' 0-4-4Ts built by the LSWR, 95 were constructed at Nine Elms between 1897 and 1906, whilst the last 10 examples emerged from Eastleigh in in 1911.

Left: A pleasing rear three-quarter view of Class M7 0-4-4T No. 676 being turned at Waterloo in March 1921. This locomotive was the last of the original batch of 25 'M7s' built by the LSWR workshops at Nine Elms and delivered between February and December 1897. This batch (Nos. 242-256 and 667-676) had cost £1,580 each to construct, and the decision to build them at Nine Elms had been taken after sub-contractors failed to submit satisfactory quotations for the class. Drummond had been authorised to sub-contract the construction of 20 large passenger tanks to his own design at an estimated cost of £1,600 per engine, but in 1896 the lowest quote submitted had exceeded this figure by nearly £800! The order was thus increased to 25 and the decision taken to construct the engines in the Company's own workshops. Of the 105 examples built, just two survive today: No. 30245 in the care of the National Railway Museum, and No. 30053, which arrived at the Swanage Railway in 1987 after repatriation from preservation in the United States of America, whence the engine had been shipped following withdrawal from service in June 1964 as the last working member of the class.

Above: Standing against the rail-built bufferstops adjacent to the Locomotive Foreman's Office in February 1915 is Drummond Class L12 4-4-0 No. 422, built for express passenger duties in 1904. Sister engine No. 421 gained notoriety in 1906 in the severe accident at Salisbury, when it rounded the curve west of the station at excessive speed, with disastrous consequences. The hoarding in the left background proclaims:: "CANTERBURY Theatre of Varieties, NON-STOP PROGRAMME FROM 6.30 DAILY, PICTURES AND VARIETIES". On the right is No. 479, an Adams Radial 4-4-2T, built in 1883. These fine 4-4-2Ts, used on suburban services until displaced after 1897 by Class M7 0-4-4Ts, formed a class of 71 engines delivered between 1883 and 1885, and their survival to this date was largely a result of the heavy demands of wartime traffic. This picture was taken during No. 479's last year of service. At the Grouping, 49 examples survived, of which 17 were regarded as derelict as a result of years of neglected maintenance. Remarkably, three examples survived into BR days as the only suitable engines for operating the sharply-curved Axminster-Lyme Regis branch, in Dorset, from where they were not displaced until 1961. LSWR No. 488 (as BR No. 30583) was withdrawn from service in July 1961 and preserved by the Bluebell Railway, in Sussex, where the engine can still be seen today

Right: The crew of Drummond Class T9 4-4-0 No. 304 pause for the photographer at Waterloo in March 1921. No. 304 was a member of a very successful class of 66 engines built between 1899 and 1901 for the Company's express passenger duties, a role they fulfilled in great style. No. 304 was one of the final batch of 15 examples built at Nine Elms works, and delivered between December 1900 and October 1901 at a cost of £2,685 each. In 1918 the LSWR decided to modernise the Drummond 4-4-0s of the L12, S11 and T9 classes by fitting superheated boilers and No. 304 was one of the first 'T9s' so treated, in 1922. The locomotive is pictured here in original condition. In SR days No. 304 was one of several 'T9s' to be paired with six-wheeled tenders for working over former SECR lines, although this view shows No. 304's original 4,000-gallon capacity double-bogie tender. These engines were very popular with footplatemen and they were extremely long-lived, the last working engines surviving as late as 1961. A single 'T9' survives, BR No. 30120, owned by the National Railway Museum and based on the Mid Hants Railway.

Above: Standing at Salisbury station in July 1922 is Adams Class X2 'Highflyer' No. 586, in charge of the newly-inaugurated Cardiff-Brighton through train, which was formed of GWR or LBSCR stock on alternate days.. No. 586 was one of a class of 20 engines (Numbered 577-596) and built at Nine Elms between June 1890 and May 1892. Designed by Adams to supersede his earlier '135', '445' and '460' class 4-4-0s, the 'X2s' were themselves subsequently displaced by Drummond's 'T9' 4-4-0s, introduced 1899-1901, after which the 'Highflyers' were relegated to secondary duties. Adams built four different classes of 'Highflyer' 4-4-0s, two with 7ft 1in diameter driving wheels, and two with 6ft 7in wheels, the latter intended for working the steeply graded route between Salisbury and Exeter. Of the 6ft 7in (Class T3) series, No. 563 (built in 1893) is preserved as part of the National Collection by the National Railway Museum, at York. In mid-1925, No. 586 was stationed at Salisbury with sister engines Nos. 580 and 592; No. 586 was usually employed working the Bournemouth West services. During the Second World War, this locomotive earned the distinction of being the last survivor of this elegant class, No. 586 working until November 1942, when after spending its last days as shed pilot at Eastleigh the locomotive was finally withdrawn and condemned for scrap The 4-4-0 had recorded an accumulated mileage of 1,323,177.

LSWR SUBURBAN SCENES

The suburban system of the LSWR was virtually complete by the time of the opening of the connecting line from the West London Railway at Kensington, to Richmond, via Hammersmith and Kew. The line curved from the WLR, mid-way between Kensington station and Uxbridge Road station. The distance from Kensington to the LSWR station at Hammersmith (Grove Road) was little more than one mile and the line opened on January 1 1869. The metals curved under Shepherd's Bush Road and the Hammersmith & City Railway (Metropolitan Railway & GWR) to reach the new station before contin-

uing towards Gunnersbury. The contemporary service offered by horse-drawn buses cannot have been either fast or comfortable and the LSWR thereby provided a reasonable alternative. Since there was a more direct route between Waterloo and Richmond the LSWR was clearly seeking to capture traffic from the intermediate stations; even so, the service cannot have been

described as rapid, the eight miles from Waterloo to Hammersmith taking more than 30 minutes, whilst the 10 miles from the LSWR's 'City' station at Ludgate Hill took 45 minutes! Extension of the District Railway to Hammersmith - and more significantly, its electrification in 1906 - seriously affected the LSWR's traffic. At this time, many of the major Companies operated cross-London services, but many of these were withdrawn, never to restart, during cuts in services caused by the First World War. The Hammersmith service was reduced in 1915 and ceased altogether in June 1916.

Below, left: The Hammersmith branch diverged from the Waterloo-Brentford and Hounslow line beyond Chiswick station and curved through Gunnersbury East Junction, shown here in July 1916.

Below, right: Hammersmith (Grove Road) station in July 1916, pictured after closure as part of wartime reductions in train services. The crossover was provided to enable engines to run round their trains, for the station featured both through and reversing services. The advertisements on the station all promote the LSWR's services, although dimly visible in the gloom beneath the canopy is a Roll of Honour, presumably recording the names of company servants who had lost their lives in the war thus far.

Left: On the branch from Kensington, the LSWR station station at Shepherd's Bush is pictured in July 1916, shortly after closure. Not only have the lamps been removed but the gates from the footbridge are firmly locked. The track was subsequently lifted and whilst the station was abandoned, its increasingly dilapidated remains survived into the 1950s. At this time, the war on the Western Front was at a critical stage and at such a perilous time it is difficult to comprehend quite why the LSWR commissioned these pictures to record the closure of a relatively minor route.

THE
LSWR SIGNALLING SCHOOL
WIMBLEDON

THE safe operation of trains on any railway depends on the teamwork of all railwaymen, from platelayers to express locomotive drivers, but signalmen have always carried a particularly heavy burden of responsibility. From the smallest cabin on a remote branch line to the huge signalboxes at main line termini such as Waterloo, the signalman was responsible for the safe passage of traffic through his section. His skills and training were of paramount importance and the pre-Grouping main line companies all had their own special training schemes. In northern England, the Lancashire & Yorkshire Railway used a large model railway which featured all the signalling practices employed on its system, and this model installation was frequently featured in the railway press of the era.

The LSWR's Signalling School, at Wimbledon, was rather different however, and whilst it also followed the LYR principle of training railwaymen in an academic, rather than a working environment, it generally used full-size equipment in its instruction, rather than models. In July 1921 the LSWR hosted a visit to its Signalling School by the Institution of Railway Signal Engineers, for which LSWR Signal & Telegraph Superintendent, W.J. Thorrowgood mounted a special display of equipment. A photographer from the *Topical Press Agency* was amongst the visitors to the exhibition, and his pictures illustrate this section.

In the August 1921 issue of *The Railway Magazine*, an article had been published describing the work of the LSWR Signalling School, and to enhance the interest of these photographs, the article is reproduced in part here, courtesy of *The Railway Magazine*. Only minor deletions have been made to the text of the article, where it relates to photographs not published in this book.

"Signalling Schools are now a feature of training systems of all railways, but that installed by the London and South Western Railway at Wimbledon differs in certain respects from most of the others, and includes several interesting

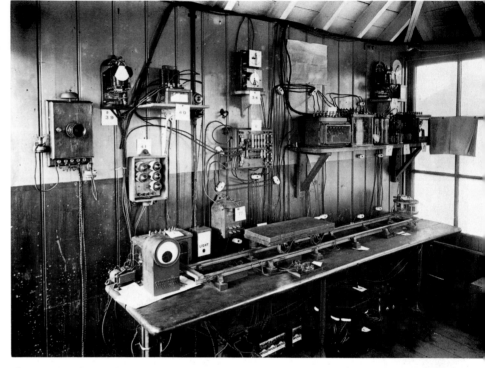

Above: This picture depicts part of the simulated signal box created in the upper floor of the LSWR's Signalling School, at Wimbledon, as laid out for the July 1921 visit by members of the Institution of Railway Signal Engineers. The small number labels, reminiscent of Lot numbers at an auction, were provided to help visitors identify various pieces of equipment. The miniature piece of track and small wagon enabled trainee signalmen to be instructed in the operation of track circuitry. The LSWR's standard AC and DC track circuit relays on the shelf adjacent to the window controlled the mechanical Sykes' 'lock and block' operations in the lever frame.

features. In connection with the School, lectures are given periodically on such subjects as "Alternating Current Track Circuit," "Automatic Train Control," etc. The School has, therefore, its lecture and theoretical study side as well as its practical and training aspects.

The distinctive feature of the School, as compared with others, is that all the illustrations or demonstrations are given by specimens of the actual apparatus in use on the line. A further distinctive feature is that all the details of the apparatus are open or available to sight and touch, so that the technical parts can be seen and watched during their operation. This has been made a specially marked feature to give those in the technical branch full opportunity of examining, handling, and studying the apparatus and its working. A telephone circuit has been fitted up in the upper room with two instruments conn-

ected to it, for testing and examination by the younger staff.

In the upper room of the school a cabin is fitted up with apparatus as used on the London and South Western Railway. The Sykes' system is represented by three sections of Sykes' "lock and block" instruments and bells, together with point and plunger locking, key releases, track circuit control, treadle releases, with actual mechanical and electrically operated signals fitted with Company's electric replacers, all fitted to the standard pattern mechanical levers and mechanical interlocking.

At the back of the box is arranged a miniature railway, divided into track circuited sections, with treadle contacts applied. The Company's standard pattern direct current and alternating current track circuit relays seen on the shelf above control the mechanical and Sykes' "lock and block" operations in

the signal frame. Entirely separate from the above is a set of Preece's three wire electric block instruments as used on about 600 miles of the railway. There is also a set of No. 6 tablet instruments to demonstrate the latest system of single line working.

On the ground floor is located the usual mechanical interlocking and undergear, also an electric signal replacer. In addition there is a set of No.1 and a set of No. 3 tablet instruments, completing the examples of all systems in general use on this railway.

The whole of the apparatus is well illustrated and described by circuit diagrams, instructions etc., provided in the School for the use of those who wish to study the various apparatus or practice the operation or working of the various systems.

When new or or novel apparatus is to be introduced into for service on the line, it is tried in the School and demonstrations given to the staff who will be responsible for its working or to others interested.

Staff engaged in technical work have appreciated the opportunities for experiment and trial thus given, as have many members of the operating branches of the service. The desire to master the details of the operations by some of the Traffic Staff has been shown by their staying in the signal box until as late as 9p.m. (summer time). On two or three occasions the Superintendent of the Line's staff have tried problems in the School to see if the solutions proposed were practicable.

One great advantage of a school like this kind is that the operation can be seen as a whole, which cannot be done in a working signal box, as the signalman only sees the working at the two ends of the sections. Then, in a signal box the safety of the traffic is predominant and practice is a long, and often an impossible process, while in the School this does not apply. Further, the principles upon which the systems depend can be more easily seen and understood in a school arranged for the purpose.

The working of railways in the future will undoubtedly call for men of varied and wide knowledge and experience, and many of the companies have provided signalling and operating schools where the principles of movements of

Above: The electric point movement due to be used by the LSWR at Feltham Gravitation Yard, pictured here at the July 1921 exhibition. The mechanism, in the shallow pit to the left of the point blades, surprised visitors, as it could be operated very rapidly (20 times in a 15-second period) and several attempts to put the movement out of order were without success.

traffic can be studied. Generally a keen interest has been exhibited, especially by the younger members of the staffs of the railways, who appear to rise to the occasion.

The Chief Engineer has taken a very great interest in the institution and progress of the School, and Mr Thorrowgood, who has been ably assisted by his Technical and Supervisory Staff at Wimbledon, has devoted considerable time to the arrangement and details of the scheme.

It is intended to arrange a series of lectures and demonstrations on various subjects connected with railway work next session, and two members of the Superintendent of the Line's office have undertaken to assist students of the operating branches in the rules and regulations of traffic working.

THE lines of what became known after 1899 as the South Eastern & Chatham Railway were noteworthy in including the two earliest railways to operate in the South of England. These were the Canterbury & Whitstable Railway, which opened on May 3 1830, three months before the Liverpool & Manchester Railway, (opened on September 15 that year) and the London & Greenwich Railway, which opened in stages, initially on February 12 1836 (from Spa Road Bermondsey, to Deptford) the Company's trains finally reaching Greenwich on Christmas Eve 1838. This was the first railway in London, and being constructed throughout on viaducts, it set a precedent for other companies to follow in major cities everywhere.

The South Eastern Railway, between London and Dover, was authorised in 1836 and opened throughout in 1844, although at this time Parliament was rather suspicious of these 'new-fangled' railways, for inevitably, their construction in towns and cities involved the demolition of some property. Consequently, Parliament insisted that SER trains should use the tracks of the London & Croydon Railway (the LBSCR after 1846) since MPs could not envisage the need for a second railway route into the capital from the south. Thus, the SER enjoyed running powers over the London & Greenwich Railway (the operation of which it took over in 1845) and the future LBSCR, which built the line to Redhill, but which had to sell to the SER that part of the route between Coulsdon (South) and Redhill which continued via Tonbridge to the present main line.

The railway network expanded gradually in the London suburban area and in Kent, and in 1864 the line from London Bridge was extended to a West End terminus at Charing Cross, which necessitated

Above: Taken in 1851, this must be one of the first railway photographs ever produced. It shows South Eastern Railway 4-2-0 No. 13 *Folkstone*, on display at the Great Exhibition of 1851, held in Hyde Park. Also exhibited was the GWR's broad gauge 4-2-2 *Lord of the Isles,* and a pair of LNWR locomotives. No. 136 *Folkstone* was brand new at the time of the exhibition, having been built that year to Crampton's patent by Robert Stephenson & Co. Ltd., of Newcastle upon Tyne. The name *Folkstone* was removed in 1869, when the engine was rebuilt as a more orthodox 2-4-0, in which form it survived until 1892 on secondary branch line duties.

the payment of a considerable amount of compensation to St Thomas's Hospital, which had to be relocated. Two years later the SER opened a new City terminus at Cannon Street and in 1868 the present main line between Tonbridge and Chislehurst, via Sevenoaks, was opened.

In the meantime, the railways in Kent, which the SER had hitherto regarded as its own, were under threat by the arrival on the scene in 1858 of the East Kent Railway; in 1859 this Company was renamed the London Chatham & Dover Railway. In 1860, by obtaining running powers, the LCDR was operating between Victoria and Bromley and only a year later reached Dover Harbour via Chatham and Canterbury. The LCDR expanded rapidly, with an independent line into London and a City terminus at Holborn Viaduct, bringing intense competition with the SER.

This resulted in the construction of branches which penetrated absurdly into each other's territory, such as the SER line to Chatham Central (actually Rochester) and the LCDR line to Greenwich. Both these routes were destined to have short lives and closed in the years after 1899, when the rival companies became jointly administered by the newly-formed South Eastern & Chatham Railway Companies Managing Committee. Thereafter, the SECR was rather better-managed than its

predecessors, even if its suburban trains left much to be desired in terms of passenger comfort. By 1922, the last year of the SECR's independent existence, it had 625 route miles of track, 724 locomotives, 3,805 passenger stock vehicles and 11,461 goods vehicles. In the previous 12 months, the Company had carried nearly 50 million passengers, a figure roughly equivalent to the current UK population of 55 million people - a powerful indication of railway business at this time.

Right: An 1867 view of Charing Cross (opened in 1864), clearly showing the extent of the ill-fated overall roof, which collapsed in 1905. The locomotive is an early Cudworth 2-4-0, which had spring-balanced safety valves on the dome and further safety valves on the firebox. Note also the primitive cab, effectively no more than a vertical spectacle plate, giving precious little shelter, typical of those early days when the welfare of the crew seemed of little concern to British railway companies. The City terminus at Cannon Street had platform lamps similar to those shown here, but fortunately, its roof was not defective.

Left: Another very early railway photograph, this time depicting Dover Pier and its railway terminus, in 1867. Two cross-Channel ferries, with enormous paddle wheels, are lying alongside the pier, whilst a train stands beneath the overall roof. The ships were owned by the London Chatham & Dover Railway, which had recently secured the Royal Mail contract, a development which prompted the SER to transfer its own sailings to its own harbour at Folkestone.

Right: The Admiralty Pier at Dover circa 1897, following the extension of the pier by approximately 2,000ft and the demolition of the station building in favour of a much lower profile shelter for cross-Channel passengers. The paddle steamer berthed on the western side of the pier (and apparently being coaled by the small crane) is the LCDR's PS *Calais-Douvres*, built in 1889 for the convenience of British visitors to the Paris Exhibition of that year. She was the second LCDR ship to bear that name but only survived in railway ownership to 1900. In that year the vessel was acquired by Liverpool & Douglas Steamers Ltd; she subsequently passed to the Isle of Man Steam Packet Company and was broken up in 1909. By this time, the SER was operating the Dover mail train and the locomotive pictured is a Stirling 4-4-0. Dover was also used by ships of the Belgian State Railways working on the route to Ostend, and after 1899,with the days of feuding between the SER and LCDR at an end, the facilities at Dover Harbour were much rebuilt and extended during the SECR days of unified management.

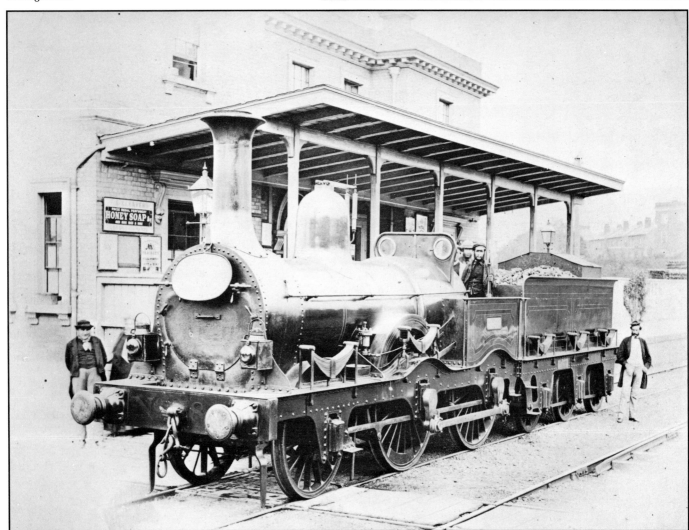

Above: This SER 2-4-0 is one of the early members of the Cudworth '118' Class engines; later examples were fitted with additional safety valves on the raised firebox and a less primitive smokebox door arrangement. Also noteworthy is the livery (probably applied by the makers) with two panels of lining on the tender side; this was unusual for at this time three panels was more common. The locomotive is standing at Erith station on the 1849 North Kent line to Gravesend, and whilst the number cannot be defined, this is probably one of the Vulcan Foundry-built series (Nos. 185-196) constructed in 1860. This picture gives a very clear indication of the highly primitive weatherboard (it cannot be described as a 'cab!') which afforded minimal protection for the footplatemen. Despite an apparent lack of concern for their working conditions by their employers, the beautifully clean condition of this locomotive is an impressive tribute indeed to the pride with which Victorian railwaymen cared for their engines.

Below: An interesting overall view of the LCDR's Ramsgate Harbour station, in June 1926. This station was reached through a tunnel on a 1 in 75 falling gradient, which on occasions caused trains to approach at too high a speed, overshoot the bufferstops and come to rest in the street! Close examination of this photograph reveals that the train engine standing adjacent to the right-hand platform is fitted for oil burning, as indicated by the long cylindrical twin tanks fitted in what would normally be the tender coalspace. The engine is one of four Stewarts Lane Class E1 4-4-0s so-fitted in June 1926, as a consequence of the miners strike and General Strike, shortly before the rationalisation of Thanet's railways was complete. A result of this was the closure of this station, and the transfer of services to the present Ramsgate station, on July 2 1926. The site was subsequently used for a fun fair. The 'E1' 4-4-0s were quite remarkable performers and some examples survived until the end of steam traction on Kent coast lines in 1961. The 'E1s' evolved because of the transference of Continental boat train traffic to Victoria in 1920, for the bridges on LCDR lines would not permit the use of the powerful Class L 4-4-0. Hence, in 1918, Class E 4-4-0 No. 179 of 1908 entered Ashford Works for rebuilding with a larger firebox, high-degree superheating and the most up to date front-end design. This conversion was so successful that ten more of the 'E' class were similarly rebuilt, whilst 21 of the similar, but older Class D 4-4-0s were likewise rebuilt as Class D1. Their performance, if anything, probably eclipsed that of the 1914 Class L 4-4-0s, for they were capable of taking trains up the steep gradient through the tunnel at Ramsgate, through the cliffs, without rear-end assistance. Note also the candy-striped bathing machines, neatly aligned close to the promenade, or close to the waters edge, where diffident bathers could creep out and dip a toe in the English Channel!

Left: On May 31 1937, a suburban train from the Otford line pauses at the old Swanley Junction station, part of which still survives (at the time of going to press) as a builders yard. This was the junction of the lines to Chatham and Otford, where the routes to Maidstone and Sevenoaks parted company. The station had been opened as Sevenoaks Junction in 1862, but was more appropriately renamed nine years later. In 1937, a simpler replacement station was under construction 21 chains west of this location (beyond the junction) to eliminate the need for a four-platform facility. The footbridge and large island platform canopies were later additions to the original LCDR station. This station closed on April 16 1939, when services were transferred to the new station.

17

Below: This promenade railway, to the Naval Dockyard at Dover, opened in 1918, thereby giving rail access to both sides of the harbour, and although it was a single track route, passing loops were provided, as shown here, to increase line capacity. The connection with the main line at the former Harbour station, was made via the Prince of Wales Pier, to the east of the Admiralty Pier. After the First World War, the Admiralty used their dockyard for breaking up obsolete ships, until it withdrew from Dover in 1925, after which a private shipbreaker occupied the site. Following development of the Kent coalfield, trains of coal for export were run over this railway for a short time. After 1939, the Admiralty resumed possession 'for the duration' and naval stores trains ran again along the Dover seafront. Ship-breaking resumed after the war and trains along the promenade predominantly carried scrap metal. In 1951, the awkward 'back-shunt' to the Prince of Wales Pier was eliminated, the demolition of adjacent property having enabled the creation of a direct link. With the conversion of the cross-Channel ferries to oil burning and the loss of export coal trade, most of the latter-day rail traffic consisted of oil tank wagons, but redevelopment of the Eastern Docks brought about closure of this little-known line in 1964. In this photograph, taken on August 26 1937, a thoughtless motorist and his careless parking has brought SECR Class P 0-6-0T and its train to a halt. Although this sort of thing undoubtedly did happen, the presence of the Topical Press photographer was rather coincidental and it is likely that the one-time favourite 'Austin Seven' was thus parked for his benefit. 'P' Class 0-6-0Ts are preserved on the Bluebell and Kent & East Sussex Railways.

Right: A remarkable photograph at Upper Sydenham station, on the former LCDR branch to Crystal Palace, opened in 1865 in an attempt to steal some of the lucrative Palace traffic from the LBSCR. The branch was closed for a time during both world wars and during the Second World War, land adjacent to neighbouring Longton Avenue was used after 1940 for the dumping of bomb rubble and by May 17 1946, when this picture was taken, around 100,000 tons of spoil had been deposited adjacent to the station. Services had only resumed two months earlier, but the 100ft high bomb rubble dump was unstable and threatening to engulf the station, as illustrated by the disturbance on the up platform. Single line operation over the down line was instituted until teams of railwaymen shored up the rubble to prevent further damage to the station. The Nunhead-Crystal Palace (High Level) branch closed first on January 1 1917, reopening on March 1 1919, then closed again from May 22 1944 to March 4 1946; it closed permanently on September 20 1954.

Above: A rather eerie view of the sadly deserted LCDR terminus at Crystal Palace
on October 23 1954, following closure of the branch from Nunhead on September
20 that year - the first SR electrified line to close. This rather grand and imposing
station, designed in the Italianate style by E.M. Barry, was marginally nearer the
Crystal Palace than the competing LBSCR station, and the splendid subway
beneath the road connecting the LCDR/LBSCR station with the Palace is still intact
and opened for display for a few days each year by the Crystal Palace Foundation.
The Crystal Palace which the LCDR station served was destroyed by fire in 1936.
This building had been constructed in 1854, using parts of the dismantled Hyde
Park exhibition building of 1851.

LONDON BRIGHTON & SOUTH COAST RAILWAY

ALTHOUGH the history of the LBSCR dates back to 1839, the name did not come into being until 1846 with the merger of the London & Brighton Railway and the London & Croydon Railway. Apart from a large coverage of suburban lines serving London, it eventually had lines covering much of Surrey and Sussex, while its main coast routes stretched from St. Leonards in the east to Portsmouth in the west. The LSWR had a working agreement covering the LBSCR line between Havant and Portsmouth, but this was not achieved peacefully, for when the LSWR Portsmouth Direct Line reached Havant at the end of 1858, the LBSCR prevented it proceeding further and the matter was taken to litigation. LSWR trains

were permitted through by the end of January 1859 but there followed a senseless price-cutting war until August, when an agreement was made to pool receipts. At the time, LBSCR trains from London had to reverse at Brighton and follow the length of the West Coast line. A more direct line to Portsmouth came with the 1863 opening of the Mid Sussex Line (via Horsham) but it was still a longer way round than the LSWR route. From 1880 the LBSCR and LSWR began jointly working the Portsmouth-Isle of

Wight ferries, hitherto privately owned. At its eastern extremity, the LBSCR had uneasy relations with the SER, whose line it joined beyond St. Leonards at the picturesquely named Bo Peep Junction. The narrow profile of the tunnel thence to Hastings meant that, although double track, only one train could pass through at a time.

The LBSCR obtained powers to electrify its system in 1903. Because much of the electrical equipment was of German

Above: The early locomotive history of the LBSCR is somewhat confused. First section of the line to open was the London & Croydon Railway, which used the tracks of the London & Greenwich Railway to gain access to London Bridge. Meanwhile, the London & Brighton Railway had been authorised, as had also the South Eastern Railway, and as these companies were compelled by Parliament originally to share the same tracks, it was decided to pool locomotives and rolling stock under a Joint Committee, but this was a short-lived arrangement and was subsequently dissolved, and the Croydon and Brighton Railways were merged as the London Brighton & South Coast Railway, in 1846. Among the most reliable of the early engines were those from Sharp Brothers of Manchester. This example,No. 45 (ex Joint Committee No. 88) was built as a 2-2-2 tender locomotive in 1844 and then rebuilt as a 2-2-2 well tank in

1851. It was involved in a strange accident in 1855, whilst hauling empty stock from New Cross to London Bridge, when it was inadvertently diverted into a siding and its poor brakes prevented it stopping, with the result that it fell from the viaduct into College Street below, where Guys Hospital is situated. Fortunately, it was little damaged and as its crew had jumped clear in time, they escaped injury. Following this incident, Driver Taunton continued to drive the engine after it had been repaired and, perhaps with visions of a quieter life, accompanied the engine when it was sold to the as-yet uncompleted Colne Valley & Halstead Railway in 1860. The CV HR was completed by 1863, but it is likely that the use of No 45 on its metals was short-lived, as three new Manning Wardle 2-4-0Ts were in service for the line's completion. Nevertheless, an early photograph of this engine at work on the CVHR does exist.

Left: A specially posed view of 2-2-2 locomotive No 284, photographed in August 1874. It has marked similarities with No 45, having been built by Sharp Brothers in 1847 as No 83 and renumbered 284 on the duplicate list in 1873. After two further renumberings the locomotive was withdrawn from service eight years later. Another of the class, No. 82, attained some degree of fame when it was deliberately derailed at Newmarket Arch (between Falmer and Lewes) causing the death of the driver and three passengers - an early example of mindless hooliganism. The suspect, never convicted, was a simple-minded youth who may or may not have realised the consequences of his action. This class of engines often worked between Brighton and Tunbridge Wells and judging by the number of station staff, this view may have been taken at Lewes.

origin, only the South London Line (London Bridge-Victoria) and the two routes to Crystal Palace had been electrified before the war. Its overhead current system, described in advertising as the 'Elevated Electric', was replaced in SR days by the LSWR third rail system. With its prestige route to Brighton, it was an early advocate

Above: A charming, early view of Carshalton station, opened in 1868 together with the line between Peckham Rye and Sutton, two years after the link between London Bridge and Peckham Rye had opened for business. This station should not be confused with Carshalton Beeches (between West Croydon and Sutton) opened in 1906 as Beeches Halt, for railmotor services, and which only attained its current name and status in 1925, with the opening of the short-lived 'Elevated Electric' extension to Sutton. Both routes were electrified using the third rail system, in 1929. At least six station staff were on duty at Carshalton when this picture was taken, and note the shingle ballast, which was woefully inadequate as trains became heavier. An interesting point for railway modellers is the single lever in the 'six foot'.

of Pullman Car luxury. It has to be admitted that its main line carriages were not as good as those of the LSWR or SECR but suburban travel on the LBSCR was infinitely better than on the SECR.

It relied on contractor-built locomotives until 1852 when J.C. Craven was appointed Locomotive Superintendent. The variety of his designs was astonishing but William Stroudley, who held that office from 1870 to 1889, imposed a remarkable degree of standardisation, in advance of similar measures taken by Churchward on the GWR. In consequence, the locomotive fleet was generally more modern than that of the LSWR or SECR, although no LBSCR designs were perpetuated after 1923. In spite of the extensive electrification of its lines, of the locomotives which came into SR ownership, 63% of LBSCR engines survived at Nationalisation, compared with 58% and 57% respectively for the LSWR and SECR. In 1922 the LBSCR had a route mileage of 431, a locomotive fleet of 615, there were 2,604 passenger vehicles and 10,357 goods vehicles and it had carried more than 56 million passengers in the previous year.

Below: A pleasant view of Billinton Class B4 4-4-0 No. 61, built in 1901 and originally named *Ladysmith*. Several of the class had names associated with the then recent Boer War. Photographed in July 1922, it is coupled to the Brighton-Cardiff through train. There seem to be a large number of railwaymen in attendance for what was presumably the inaugural westbound train of July 10 that year. Note also the 'roofer', watching the proceedings from his lofty 'perch!' There were 33 engines of this class, built between 1899 and 1902, eight at Brighton works, the remainder by Sharp Stewart & Co. of Glasgow, hence their unofficial nickname of 'Scotchmen'. These engines succeeded Stroudley's 'Gladstone' 0-4-2s and Billinton's earlier 4-4-0s on main line duties, remaining the largest tender engines on the LBSCR until the appearance of the first series of Marsh 'Atlantics' in 1906. The last B4 4-4-0s survived until 1951. The steam traction record for the London-Brighton line was attained by 'B4' No. 70 *Holyrood* in 1903, with a down run of 48 3/4 minutes, at an average speed of 62 mph, but with a lightweight load of only three Pullman cars and a van behind the tender.

Right: The last survivor of William Stroudley's 'Gladstone' Class 0-4-2s was also the last-built example, No. 172. Originally named *Littlehampton* in 1891, this was the only member of its class to survive to 1933. Such was the popularity of the class that in the late 1920s the Stephenson Locomotive Society launched an appeal for the preservation of the pioneer engine, No. 214 *Gladstone*, the funds collected meeting the cost of cosmetic restoration; the SR donated the engine itself. No. 214 had latterly run as SR No. B618, surviving until 1927, after which it became Britain's first privately preserved standard gauge locomotive. *Gladstone* was exhibited initially at Brighton and, as shown here, on May 14 1927 at Waterloo, in company with the new Maunsell express 4-6-0, No. E850 *Lord Nelson*. Special platform tickets were issued for the occasion. *Gladstone* went to the York Railway Museum at the end of that month. In BR days, ownership was transferred to the British Transport Commission and then in 1975 No. 214 was transferred to the new National Railway Museum. York.

Left: A driver explains *Gladstone's* various cab fittings to two neatly uniformed schoolboys during the May 1927 exhibition at Waterloo. The simplicity of the cab layout is remarkable! *Gladstone* was built in 1882 and covered nearly 1,350,000 miles during its 45-years active life, the highest recorded mileage of any engine of the class. Until superseded at the end of the 19th century, the class of 36 examples was the LBSCR's principal express class. The engines were unusual in their use of large diameter leading driving wheels: other locomotive engineers avoided this practice due to concerns about unsteady riding and safety. However, the Stroudley 0-4-2s rode easily at speed and showed great power for their size in mastering heavy trains on the difficult upgrade start from Victoria. In the summer of 1982, *Gladstone* returned to its home territory when it was loaned for exhibition purposes to the Bluebell Railway, in connection with celebrations to commemorate the centenary of the Lewes & East Grinstead Railway.

Below: This remarkable early picture of Ryde Esplanade station in the early years after the opening of the line was presumably taken from the top floor of a nearby hotel. At the time, the pier toll was 1d and a horse tramway ran to the Pier Head. This had originally started in the streets but with the extension of the railway there was no longer any need for it to run, other than on the Pier. The octagonal roundhouse adjacent to the station building was a Booking Office for the steamer service at this time, the similar building to the left performing the function of a waiting room. Note the signals at the end of the platform, towards the Pier Head, which are of Saxby & Farmer type, with large lamps below the signal arms. Later, this view was impossible for five trees were planted beside the kerb adjoining the station building, and by the turn of the century they had grown quite large. The distant arms denote which platform the train is to occupy at the Pier Head.

THE ISLE OF WIGHT

THE Isle of Wight is not large, but nevertheless its railway history is complex, and despite its size a remarkable number of companies emerged. By the 1923 Grouping, these were: the Isle of Wight Railway, the Isle of Wight Central Railway and the Freshwater, Yarmouth & Newport Railway.

By this time the previous smaller companies formed parts of the IWR or IWCR. Also, the FYNR had at one time been worked by the IWCR but it disagreed over rates in 1913 and thus bought two engines and some second-hand coaches of its own. This railway connected with the LSWR's Lymington-Yarmouth ferry service of the LSWR, but the Company nevertheless had an inflated idea of its importance, since at the Grouping it held out for higher compensation on the grounds that a Solent Tunnel scheme had been mooted. Its protests were in vain and it was absorbed in the SR, albeit belatedly, in August 1923. Since the island Railways probably did not have sufficient funds to build the Pier extension, a half-mile in length from Ryde St. Johns Road to Ryde Pier Head, this was funded jointly by the LBSCR and LSWR and that part of the island's rail system was

therefore their joint property. The new line, which involved tunnelling under the Esplanade, was opened in 1880 at which time the two companies took over the Portsmouth-Ryde ferry service. The Isle of Wight Central Railway should receive special mention as it was an 1887 amalgamation of the Cowes & Newport Railway, the Isle of Wight (Newport Junction) Railway and the Ryde & Newport Railway. The last mentioned line diverged from the Ryde line at Smallbrook Junction to pass through Ashey, Haven Street, Wootton, Whippingham and Newport. This line has been singled out because Haven Street is the home of the Isle of Wight Steam Railway, which operates the line to Wootton in the summer months. Fortunately, Haven Street station survived intact and has been restored to a very high standard.

Above: The Topical Press Agency sent a photographer to record Freshwater station on August 12 1931. It seems an odd subject to cover in its own right - perhaps the Agency had another event to record in the Island? The station was improved by the SR in 1927, when the layout was remodelled, with an extended platform and a new signal box. The station was a single platform terminus with run-round facility and a siding. It survives today in industrial use, the line having closed in 1953. Indeed, in BR days even before the Beeching era, most of the Isle of Wight lines were closed. Latter-day steam operations were exclusively worked by LSWR Adams Class O2 0-4-4Ts; these ceased at the end of 1966, by which time only the line from Ryde Pier Head to Shanklin survived. This was electrified during 1967 and because of clearance difficulties in the tunnel under the Esplanade, second-hand London Transport underground stock is used. It is strange to sit in one of these ancient trains and see the route maps on the walls indicating 'Ryde-Shanklin' instead of the more familiar 'Morden-Edgware'. At the time of going to press, these are now the oldest passenger coaches still in use on BR metals some of the vehicles dating back to the 1920s.

Above: A pleasing view of the PS *Merstone* from the deck of the PS *Sandown*, which were among the vessels used on the Portsmouth-Ryde crossing. The *Merstone* was built in 1928 by the Caledon Shipbuilding & Engineering Company, Dundee, which built sister steamer *Portsdown*, also for the Isle of Wight service, in 1928. *Merstone* weighed 342 tons gross and was capable of just over 13 knots; she offered saloon accommodation and also a promenade deck, the latter for the use of first class passengers. Overall passenger capacity was 723. Two larger steamers, the PS *Whippingham* and the PS *Southsea*, were built in 1930 by Fairfield Shipbuilding, of Glasgow, for the SR's Isle of Wight service, capable of carrying 1,350 passengers at 16 knots. The *Southsea* was lost during the Second World War

Left: A stern view of the PS *Freshwater*, built in 1927 by J.S. White, Cowes, and used on the Lymington-Yarmouth service. A small vessel with a capacity of only 400 passengers, and just 264 tons gross weight, she was withdrawn in 1959. In 1960-1 she entered private service, initially as the *Sussex Queen* and later as the *Swanage Queen*, but, alas, the days of the paddle steamer excursion were over and she was sold to Belgian shipbreakers in 1962.

THE Southern Railway, through its three principal pre-Grouping constituents, inherited more London terminal stations than any other of the 'Big Four' grouped companies. The stations were: **LSWR**: Waterloo; **SECR**: Cannon Street, Charing Cross, Holborn Viaduct, Blackfriars; **LBSCR/SECR**: London Bridge, Victoria.

Of these, the largest and most up-to-date was Waterloo, with 21 platforms. It had its early origins in 1848, when it had replaced the inconveniently sited Nine Elms terminus of 1838. After several extensions, a complete rebuilding commenced at the turn of the century, not to be finished until 1922. The so-called 'Windsor side' of the station had already added another six platform faces, while further rebuilding took place in 1878 and 1885. This concentrated 16 platform lines into four running lines - the original 1848 provision - but two more lines were added before the turn of the century, and a further two in 1916. The rebuilding completed in 1922 was very extensive and only the Windsor side platforms retained their original roof, from the 1885 rebuilding.

Waterloo was important for many reasons: for example, it was the principal station for Portsmouth, with its naval dockyard and Isle of Wight ferries. Other ferries (not railway owned) also ran from Southampton, where the docks area was substantially extended by the railway, providing greatly improved access for ocean liner traffic. To the west, the holiday resorts of Bournemouth, Weymouth and the West Country brought a considerable increase in summer traffic to Waterloo. The terminus also served the many military establishments in Surrey, Hampshire and Wiltshire, notably Aldershot and Salisbury Plain. In addition, it served several race courses, a shared feature with other London termini. This entailed much extra traffic at Waterloo: for instance, during one Sandown Park race meeting on the busy August Bank Holiday of 1939, there were 13 extra electric train departures and two First Class-only steam specials, in addition to traffic from other

Chapter 2: London Termini

WATERLOO

Above: Master of all he surveys - a striking image of the proud stance of the railway companies of the pre-Nationalisation years. The carefully groomed top hat and tail coat of the Waterloo Station Master is of course accompanied by pressed pinstriped trousers, an immaculate white shirt and neatly folded handkerchief, as he looks out across a curiously tranquil scene at this normally hectic London terminus. This was an era in which the authority of the Station Master was absolute and the hierachy of the railway was a proudly maintained tradition which generated and demanded respect and a determination to provide a second-to-none service.

parts of the system, such as horse box specials. It was fortunate indeed that Waterloo had the capacity to deal with extra traffic such as this at peak times. As the number of electrified lines increased, the handling of traffic at the terminus became easier, with

Above The unpretentious entrance to the station for road vehicles, cars, omnibuses, taxicabs and vans. It would be interesting to know what part of a pigs anatomy reminded the Electric Hose & Rubber Company of its 'Electric Hose' product - presumably 'nose' to complete the rhyme? This view is dated May 1922.

Above: The splendid frontage of Waterloo station on August 27 1929. Above the steps is the Victory Arch, which commemorates LSWR men killed during the First World War. There were more taxis on the London streets in those days, including some examples with immaculate whitewall tyres - and what memories are revived by the sign pointing to 'Trams in Westminster Bridge Road for all parts of South London. All night cars (Saturday nights excepted.)' The reason for the exception was that the nocturnal services were provided primarily for the press and print workers from Fleet Street, who finished work early on Saturday nights, once the Sunday newspapers were printed.

reduced requirements for releasing locomotives from the bufferstops. In steam days, most of the carriage stock was provided from Clapham Junction, although some was stabled as far afield as Weybridge.

Motive power was provided by Nine Elms, and some train engines would leave the shed for Clapham Junction where they would collect empty stock and haul it tender-first to Waterloo. The engines would remain at the bufferstops until these trains were hauled away, whereupon they were released from the platform ready to back down onto their own trains. Similar duties were carried out by some engines from train arrivals, which when released from their own trains would haul the empty stock of a later arrival from the terminus. Otherwise, light engines often coupled up in batches to run to Nine Elms, in order to reduce line occupation. The station had sidings for locomotive servicing although the turntables were only adequate for small 4-4-0s and they were little-used by the 1930s, when 'King Arthur' and 'Lord Nelson' 4-6-0s were in charge of express workings.

One of Waterloo's more noticeable features was the large signal box spanning the tracks at the country end of the station - a good vantage point for photographers. This, Waterloo A Box, had gradually been extended, the major work being completed in 1892, the lever frame being further enlarged when the approach tracks were widened and the station rebuilt. There were also B, C and D boxes, the former being the most important. All these were replaced by a new power box, opened on the Thames side of the station in October 1936, which replaced six manual boxes and introduced colour light signals. This took place a few months after the opening of the Wimbledon flyover, enabling a rearrangement of tracks to reduce conflicting movements.

In terms of passengers, Waterloo takes only second place to Liverpool Street and it is worth remembering that alone among the SR constituents in the first years of the century, Waterloo would have seen no non-bogie carriages.

Left: A very busy scene at Waterloo at holiday time. It is May 3 1912 and only Drummond engines can be seen standing at the buffer-stops. The train at Platform 2 is a suburban train for Teddington, whilst standing at Platform 3 is a Bournemouth-bound service. The 'Windsor side' of the station is concealed from the main station. Note that the small building in the foreground (probably a bookstall, at one stage) is covered with promotional holiday posters of the type which now bring very good prices at auctions! Straw 'boaters' were clearly very much in vogue - very much the England of Jerome K. Jerome!

Right: A May 1922 view of the station, showing the well-remembered Train Departure Indicator, whose operator suddenly appeared from its rear, armed with a long, hooked stick, if one of the station names had not turned to show clearly. By this time Platforms 1-6 and 16-21 were available for electric trains.

Left: An unusual visitor to Waterloo. SECR Wainwright Class C 0-6-0 No. A686 had brought in a set of the latest SECR boat train stock, for official inspection by the Company Directors. Another engine had hauled the stock out sufficiently to release No A 686 for it to run round the train, and be photographed standing at its head, as illustrated here. Although many former SECR men held high office in SR days, it was probably thought 'not the done thing' in 1923 to have one of its engines at the LSWR bufferstops at Waterloo!. This picture is dated October 1923, so the engine must have been an early repaint into SR livery.

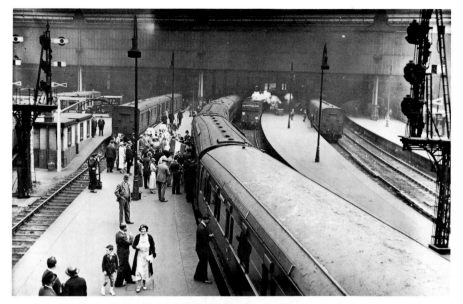

Left: A train of the so-called 'Ironclad' corridor coaches, of the LSWR, carrying roofboards which read 'Ocean Liner Express. Waterloo Southampton Docks.' The date is August 17 1934, when South African athletes were on their way home after taking part in the British Empire Games. The original Topical Press caption reads: "The scene at Waterloo station as the boat train carrying the South African athletes steamed out." Provided with captions like this, it is perhaps not surprising that the newspapers sometimes get their facts wrong!

Below: On May 29 1936, Whitsun holidaymakers throng the platforms at Waterloo, en route to the Isle of Wight. The train, carrying the Portsmouth line headcode, is hauled by SR 1924-built Class H15 4-6-0 No. 478, a Maunsell version of the powerful class originated by R.W. Urie of the LSWR. Note that by this time the Waterloo goods hoist towers are proclaiming: 'Read the News of the World, the best weekly paper.'

Left: Before the age of motorways, the railways were the best way to travel, though even then, Bank Holidays were very hectic periods. Only electric trains can be seen at the buffer stops, and note at left the circular Main Line Booking Office. The steps down to the Waterloo & City Railway and Waterloo Road still remain today. In front of the steps are seven telephone booths, while on the right is the once-familiar Nestles chocolate machine, supplying chocolate bars for 1d or 2d. Look carefully for the lady in the very midst of the throng, standing in the enquiries booth!

Below: A view showing in the distance the old signal box straddling the tracks at Waterloo. On February 20 1931, Maunsell 'Lord Nelson' Class 4-6-0 No. E 860 *Lord Hawke* enters the terminus in charge of the 'Bluebird Special', which brought Captain Malcolm Campbell back to London following his breaking of the world land speed record at Daytona Flats, USA, in his car 'Bluebird', for which achievement he later received a knighthood. Meanwhile, on the SR, later in 1931 all 'E' prefixed engines (ex LSWR and SR Eastleigh-maintained new engines) would lose their E prefix, those of SECR origin and their derivatives (such as the Maunsell 'Moguls') would lose the 'A' prefix and have instead 1000 added to their numbers. Finally, ex LBSCR engines lost the 'B' prefix and their numbers were increased by 2000. Engines on what had been termed the LSWR 'duplicate list,' which had their numbers prefixed by 0, had 3000 added to their numbers. Remarkably, although the LSWR had placed them on the duplicate list, several survived into BR ownership.

Above, left: A signalman at work in the 1892 signal box (illustrated at the top of this page), the frame of which was extended when the extra running lines were put in. The 74ft x 30ft signalbox actually had 250 levers at this time but its method of 'triple working', gave it the equivalent of having 410 levers! The frame was of Stevens design, and its interlocking was extremely comprehensive, some main line signals requiring the operation of 15 different levers.The 102 signal levers in fact operated 247 semaphore signal arms. When the new power box was installed and commissioned, this once notable Waterloo landmark was demolished.

Above, right: The work looks much easier in the 1936 power box, which was equipped with 309 miniature levers and 16 train and engine describers. The clock reveals that the 'Atlantic Coast Express' is about to depart but there is no air of urgency apparent in the signalbox. The four track diagrams seen here covered the layout as far as Vauxhall. The box was of the concrete type much favoured by the SR in the 1930s.

Above: A scene showing the Windsor side of the station in late SR days. An electric train is in the centre of the picture, formed of one of the sets built new in 1925 for work on the Eastern Section, augmented to four coaches by the insertion of a steel trailer coach. A similar set is berthed in the sidings, while at extreme left stands Class M7 0-4-4T No 249, in wartime black livery. At right, No. 21C7 *Aberdeen Commonwealth*, of the 'Merchant Navy' Class, has come on to the rear of an arrival, in readiness to haul the empty stock to Clapham Junction. The 'Pacific' will have worked in with an earlier arrival and will proceed from Clapham Junction to Nine Elms shed for servicing. As BR No. 35007, *Aberdeen Commonwealth* was rebuilt in May 1958 and was ultimately withdrawn from service in July 1967. The locomotive was scrapped at Newport in April 1968.

Left: An extraordinary scene at Waterloo station on July 19 1948, BR having announced that the whole of the track adjacent to platform 5 would be relaid between the morning and evening rush hours. Normally, such work was carried out at week-ends or at night, and the work commanded much interest. Clearly, it has attracted a large number of spectators as SR English Electric-built 350 hp diesel No. 1 (later BR 15201) one of three such engines built in 1937, manoeuvres the prefabricated track panels into position.

Right: Station Masters at the top London stations and indeed important city stations outside London, wore top hats, tail coats and white gloves for special occasions. Here we see the Waterloo Station Master chatting to the footplate crew of a 1945-built 'Merchant Navy' 4-6-2, prior to departure. Compare the 'Southern' roundel on the smokebox door with that provided initially for the class, as illustrated on the rear cover of this book. It is said that Bulleid modified the design after it was pointed out to him that the original pattern was effectively an 'upturned horsehoe' - which is traditionally a symbol of bad luck.

VICTORIA

THIS station was originally owned by the Victoria Station & Pimlico Railway, the LBSCR having subscribed two thirds of the capital for the western side of the station, while the London Chatham & Dover and Great Western Railways jointly secured a long lease for the eastern side. GWR occupancy at that time involved mixed gauge tracks. To

Right: The muddle that was Victoria station before the 1908 rebuilding. At the far side at least the LBSCR had provided a portico to enable passengers to transfer to and from horse cabs without getting wet. Indeed, there is a proliferation of horse cabs, only one horse-drawn bus being evident. The name of the Company's catering agents, Spiers and Pond, is prominent on the LCDR station. All the European stations named could be reached by means of the LCDR's own steamship service from Dover to Calais, while the LBSCR served the continent via Newhaven and Dieppe.

reach the station, the famous engineer, John Fowler, designed Grosvenor Bridge, 930 ft long and the first railway bridge over the River Thames in the London area. The LBSCR station opened in 1860 and the LCDR Joint station two years later. GWR outer suburban services via the West London Railway were never destined to make a great impact and ceased in 1915. Trains of the GNR and Midland Railways also used this side of the station until 1917. Both stations were substantially rebuilt in 1908 giving a rather more uniform appearance.

The LCDR, serving primarily East Kent and the Kent Coast, in addition to the suburbs, had an impecunious start in life, but attained some degree of respectability towards the end of its existence. Nevertheless, the rolling stock used on its suburban services was even poorer than that of the SER and when the 1923 Grouping took place, it was a prime candidate for electrification.

Former LCDR lines from both Victoria and Holborn Viaduct were electrified in 1925, to Orpington, via the main line and the Catford Loop, as was the branch from Nunhead to Crystal Palace High Level. Electrification was extended to Sevenoaks in 1935, Maidstone and Gillingham in 1939 and the Kent Coast 20 years later.

Meanwhile the LBSCR had been a very early supporter of electrification, to combat inner suburban tramway competition. The South London Line to London Bridge via Peckham Rye was electrified on the 6,600 volts AC system in 1909 and extended to Crystal Palace two years later, with a further short extension the following year, via

Above: Victoria's frontage in 1910, two years after rebuilding. Motor buses were still outnumbered by horse cabs, but note that one of the vehicles (right, middle distance) is petrol driven. Note also the District Railway station at right, since 1933 part of the unified London Underground system, but still known as the District Line. There is much interesting detail to observe in this picture, such as the carpenter's horse and cart in the foreground. The driver is doubtless busy in the station, and has left his horse with a nosebag, until his return. Note the Great Western Railway lettering above the main archway, for GWR trains used Victoria from 1863 until 1915, as described in greater detail in *GWR Reflections,* a companion volume .The exterior stonework at Victoria has been cleaned in recent years, thereby restoring its 1908 glory, although it is now less possible to appreciate its splendour because of the presence of a large covered bus station in the forecourt.

Norwood Junction, to Selhurst, where a stabling and servicing depot for the electric stock was provided. One such depot had already been built at Peckham Rye in 1909.

Below, left: A March 1930 view of the station. By this time, a modest bus station was beginning to take shape on the forecourt (compare this picture with the view shown on page 32) and the motor buses now have pneumatic tyres and covered tops. Above the former LBSCR station, the Grosvenor Hotel stands, while below the canopies can be seen a 'Southern Electric' sign, which was prominently displayed on every station served by the electric network.

Below, right The Eastern Section Booking Hall sustained some damage during the war, and it is said that a German aircraft was brought down here. This view shows the new 1951 Booking Hall, itself destined to have a relatively short life, since the area was subsequently taken over by the Continental Travel offices, and today's Booking Hall is located on the concourse of the former LBSC station.

Much of the electrical equipment was obtained from the German company AEG, hence supplies ceased during the First World War, and the final extensions to Sutton and Coulsdon were not completed until 1925, by which time it had been decided that the overhead system would be abandoned in favour of the LSWR third rail system, operating at 600 volts DC.

Third rail electrification of former LBSCR suburban lines then proceeded apace, commencing in 1928, the last overhead electric train running during the following year. With the electrification of the LBSCR suburban lines completed, the SR turned its attention to the main lines, Brighton and Worthing being reached in 1933, Eastbourne and Hastings in 1935 and the Mid

Sussex Line to Portsmouth (via Horsham and Chichester) in 1938, including branches to Littlehampton and Bognor.

Until the recent alterations to the concourse were carried out, which, reduced platform lengths, and building work over the platforms, there has been little change at Victoria, which retains much of its character and splendour.

Right: This photograph was taken to show the aftermath of a minor derailment in August 1910 but it gives a good impression of the approach to Victoria. In the immediate foreground can be seen the masts supporting the wires of the Elevated Electric system, whilst all lines to the right are those into the SECR station. At left are the LBSCR engine servicing sidings and turntable. Note the signals controlling the entrance to some of the LBSCR platforms; this was because the length of the platforms permitted two trains to occupy a platform at the same time, but the second train had to be brought to a stand as a warning of the presence of another train.

Left: A rather sad view of soldiers leaving Victoria in January 1915, on their way to Folkestone and the Western Front. The SECR is using its then best boat train stock - note the First and Second Class signs on the nearest carriage doors. The carriage about to pass beneath the bridge appears to be a Pullman Car, presumably for the officers. How many of the men waving and smiling from the drop windows, full of optimism in leaving these shores to serve King and country, failed to return? Note the overcoated gentleman on the platform, standing to attention and saluting the men as they pass. The train is leaving from Platform 8, eventually to become the 'Golden Arrow' platform. Note that the SECR and LBSCR stations at that time were totally separated by a high wall.

Above: It is January 1924 at Victoria, and passengers for Orpington will be pleasantly surprised when they reach Platform 5 and find a train of bogie stock awaiting them. The relatively quiet atmosphere indicates that this was an off-peak service, doubtless using a main line set, filling in time between main line turns. The SECR was always short of carriage sidings, so it was expedient to keep trains on the move. During peak business hours, commuters had to endure the discomfort of non-bogie stock, hence the urgency for electrification of these lines. Note the ornate platform fittings, chiefly the lamps and platform number sign poles, and the stern notice on the gate, which reads: "NOTICE To ensure the punctual departure of the trains, this barrier will be closed immediately before the advertised starting time." The uniformed ticket collector gives the impression that he would implement this rule with the utmost strictness!

Right: Over on the LBSCR side of the station, Class B4 4-4-0 No. 58, formerly named *Kitchener* when built in 1901, stands with a Newhaven Harbour boat train on January 18 1921. The elliptical-roofed boat train stock was built in 1908, the last of over 100 examples of this type of coach. The boat train was non-corridor, for the LBSCR had only one corridor coach, used on the Brighton-London Bridge 'City Limited' business train and connected to a Pullman car. The width and height of these coaches confined them to the main line, and their life on the SR was relatively short, since the loading gauge on SECR and some LSWR lines was very much less generous than that of the LBSCR. Some set trains survived until 1939, usually all First class coaches set aside for race specials. After withdrawal many of the coach bodies were grounded either for departmental use or as accommodation for Home Guard units.

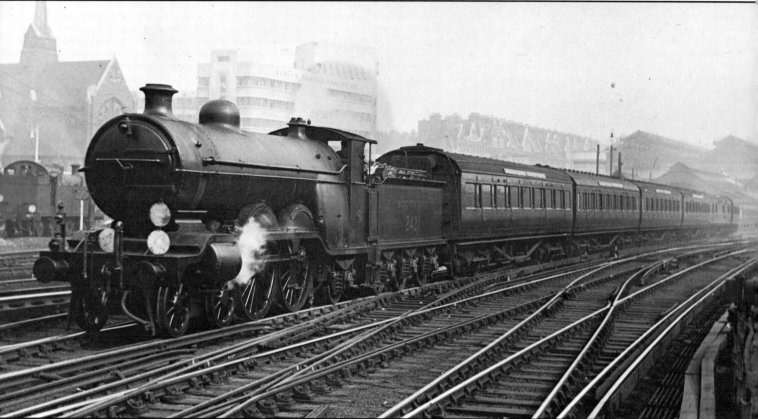

Above: A very attractive image of the inter-war boat train operations of the SR. Class H2 'Atlantic' No. 2421 *South Foreland*, first of a second series of 4-4-2s built at Brighton works in 1911, leaves Victoria about 1935 with a continental boat express bound for Newhaven Harbour. The SR gave names of well known headlands to these engines, the last of which (BR No. 32424 *Beachy Head*) survived until 1958. It has been suggested that *Portland Bill* (SR No. 2038) sounded more like a convict than a coastal feature! This series of locomotives was designed by L. B. Billinton, who succeeded D. E. Marsh as LBSCR Locomotive Superintendent in 1911. Marsh joined the LBSCR from the Great Northern Railway, and as illustrated here, his 'Atlantics' bore a passing resemblance to that company's Ivatt 4-4-2s. In 1937, No. 2421's boiler fittings and cab were reduced in height to enable the locomotive to meet the loading gauge requirements of the former SECR lines, on which some examples worked in the summer in 1938. The 'H2' class spent two years in the early part of the Second World War at Basingstoke. Most of their lives were spent on their home section, and latterly in the 1950s on the heavier Oxted line trains linking London and the coast, via Sheffield Park or Uckfield; on Saturday through services to and from Willesden, and relief Newhaven boat trains. The locomotive visible in the engine yard on the left is a Class I1X 4-4-2T, a Maunsell rebuild of Marsh's first design, at this time in use on Tunbridge Wells West line services.

Right: On March 24 1937, early Easter holiday-makers leave Victoria, bound for a 15 day tour of Italy, organised by Thomas Cook & Son. The original caption to this picture suggests that the same train will be used throughout the trip: this may have been the case on the continent, but it is unlikely that the SECR coaches went beyond the Channel port. By this time, Victoria was handling an enormous amount of continental traffic; following the 1899 agreement forming the SECR Managing Committee, a loop from the LCDR line at Bickley was opened in 1902, linked to the SER line at Orpington, enabling Victoria's boat trains to reach the more easily-graded SER line (via Tonbridge and Ashford) also providing a direct connection to Folkestone. There was inadequate space at Charing Cross to handle increased continental traffic, hence its transfer to Victoria in 1920. In this picture, a young man employed by Thomas Cook is presenting a button-hole to passengers. The coach in the foreground is one of the 1907-built composites for the through services. It is to be hoped that the lady accepting the flower secured the carriage door handle before departure!

Above: The Continental Booking Office as it was in SECR days. Remarkably, the most prominent notices are all in English, and this was unusual, for the SECR was very much a bilingual line, with notices in both English and French at stations and in main line carriages.

Left: In October 1938, the new Imperial Airways building is pictured under construction. At that time, there were only a few months of independent life remaining for the famous airline, as the Parliamentary Bill amalgamating it with British Airways Ltd (not the present company) to form the British Overseas Airways Corporation, was passed in August 1939. In front of the building, the new power signal box to take over the Victoria colour light signalling in 1939 was externally complete. In the 1980s, the BOAC (later part of the present British Airways) building has been demolished and the signal box shown here also has been replaced by a new power box covering a very wide area.

Below: On June 6 1939, an immaculately groomed LSWR Drummond Class T9 4-4-0 ,No 338, of Eastleigh, leaves Platform 17 (the westernmost platform of the former LBSCR station) with an Imperial Airways Special to Southampton Docks, run in connection with the Empire Flying Boat Service. Imperial Airways was awarded the contract for conveying mails throughout the British Empire and immediately decided to use flying boats for this service, rather than traditional aircraft, ordering 28 of the very successful *Empire* class aeroplanes from Short Brothers, regular services for passengers and mails starting in 1937. This train marked the opening of the Imperial Airways Air Terminal at Victoria, then the first in the world to have direct connection with an air base. Prior to this, the trains had run most weekdays since July 1937 from Waterloo. In 1940, under BOAC auspices, those flying boat services to continue during the war were transferred to Poole, until 1948 when they returned to Southampton for two years, after which land-based aircraft took over. The service shown here ran again in 1942, in connection with flights to West Africa, a distribution base for much Empire mail. The trains ran via Balham and Streatham Junction to Wimbledon, where they joined the LSWR main line. At that time, the train comprised a 4-4-0, perhaps two Pullman cars and a brake carriage or bogie van.

Right: Rather cramped conditions in the former LBSCR 1908 signal box at Victoria, one of a series of pictures by a *Picture Post* photographer to show life at a London station. The original caption reads: "One of the most fascinating places in the world is a great London station. No place is more packed with activity, drama, interest and anticipation. The trains are symbols of change and parting and a symbol of business activity. In one day, nearly 1,000 trains carrying 123,000 passengers pull out of Victoria station." Note the indicators (above the levers) showing whether or not North or South Ends of the platform were occupied; this illustrates the feature mentioned on page 34, whereby the 'Brighton side' platforms could hold two trains at once. Imagine the atmosphere in this signalbox at peak hour periods, with levers crashing back and forth, bells ringing, telephones to be answered and clocks to be watched - and in the midst of it all, the railwayman keeping the train register at the back of the box (left) had to ensure that all entries were accurately made.

LONDON BRIDGE

Below: SECR Wainwright Class H 0-4-4T No. 321 enters Platform 4 at London Bridge with an up Greenwich line train of non-bogie SER coaches, the low-roof coach at the head of the train indicating a vehicle of particular old age. The later-built coaches seen this train were of the type to be used subsequently by the SR in electric stock conversions. In the misty background, another Class H tank is seen approaching Platform 7 with an up train, whilst to the right of the lowered Platform 7 signal can be seen a Wainwright Class C 0-6-0, ready to haul empty stock from the Low Level station.

LONDON BRIDGE has the distinction of being the oldest terminus in London, the London & Greenwich Railway having opened as far as Deptford in 1836. The approximate site of the original terminus occupied what became the SECR Low Level terminus, between the LBSCR station and the eventual through lines of the SECR, to Charing Cross and Cannon Street. The railway approaching London Bridge was carried on viaducts, following the pattern already established by the London & Greenwich Railway. The station has been rebuilt several times and inevitably extended, thereby obliterating any trace of the original terminus. With the 1864 extension to Charing Cross, the new high level station of the SECR was reached by means of a gradient of 1 in 103, later in wet weather to provide a hazard for Bulleid 'Pacifics' on heavy commuter trains from the Kent Coast, when checked by signals. The practice in these circumstances was for an electric train to draw forward slowly to give rear end assistance. There were 11 roads on the immediate approach to the station and the platforms in SR days

Left, below: The Topical Press photographer has captured all four lines occupied at London Bridge, near Borough Market Junction Signalbox, where conflicting movements were common. This was because London Bridge (High Level) had three 'up' and three 'down' platforms, and 'up' Cannon Street trains had to cross the path of 'down' Charing Cross trains, for example. In 1922, a form of parallel working was instituted, whereby two Cannon Street trains could be passed for each Charing Cross-bound train, and this was the reason for a visit by a Topical Press Agency photographer, in May of that year. On the left is a main line train of bogie coaches heading away from the camera. The second up train (second from the left) consists of non-bogie coaches, whilst on the first down road (third from the left) is a reboilered Stirling 4-4-0, running tender-first. It is impossible to tell whether this is a passenger or an empty stock train, since the peak-hour workings were so intensive that down trains worked by engines running tender-first could often be seen, hauled even by 0-6-0s on some occasions. Southwark Cathedral can be clearly seen in this picture. These two pictures were taken between 9am and 10 am on a weekday. By 1968, the position had changed, for business has been drifting away from the City and Charing Cross was handling 120,000 passengers each day to Cannon Street's 80,000.

Right: The interior of London Bridge A signal box, at the London end of Platforms 1 and 2, on April 27 1928. Note the array of circular train describers enabling signalmen to route trains correctly. This was a 41-lever box, the smallest at London Bridge. The occasion is the equipping of the box with a microphone for train announcements to passengers. The microphone can be seen suspended between the two signalmen. One would have thought they had enough to do; perhaps the Traffic Inspector made the announcements.

Below: The station exterior in August 1929, with the relatively newly-permitted covered-top solid-tyred NS type buses awaiting passengers. The building on the left was the former SER building of 1851, whilst to the right, in the background, is the former LBSCR station built three years later. Note the large notice promoting the SR's electric services, a highly successful initiative introduced by this country's first Public Relations Officer, John Elliot, who in 1947 became the SRs last General Manager. He subsequently served as Chief Regional Officer of British Railways, Southern Region. Both buildings suffered severe bomb damage in the Second World War. Rebuilding of the station eventually followed in 1979. Road traffic now runs in the opposite direction and a covered bus station has been provided.

Right: This photograph was taken at London Bridge in very murky conditions on March 15 1934 to record the last footplate journey of Eastbourne Driver G Hall, after 46 years of service. At this time, Eastbourne had four 'Schools' 4-4-0s on its allocation, (Nos. 913-6) and this is No. 915 *Brighton*. After the 1933 electrification of the main line to Brighton, the Maunsell 2-6-0s, hitherto used on Eastbourne trains, were displaced by the seven LBSCR 4-6-4-Ts (after 1935 converted to the 'Remembrance' Class 4-6-0s) and five Brighton 'Atlantics' Within three months, the first 'Schools' 4-4-0s had arrived at Eastbourne and they were kept in such immaculate condition that they were often borrowed for special trains. This locomotive was one of the class to be fitted by Bulleid with a Lemaitre multiple-jet blastpipe and large diameter chimney: the engine was withdrawn from service in December 1962 and was scrapped at Eastleigh in November 1963.

Left, upper: A minor derailment on March 10 1948, on the up South London line tracks of the former LBSCR, serves well to illustrate the way in which London Bridge station was approached entirely by lines carried on viaducts. The thrifty railway companies rented out the arches! The Directors of the London & Greenwich Railway had conceived the idea that they could make money by converting the arches into housing, but this plan was frustrated by noise and damp! This picture features a rich array of peripheral detail for the railway modeller.

Left, below: Another minor derailment, which affected train services quite seriously. On February 15 1950, No. 35029, built in 1949 but as then unnamed, was running light from Charing Cross when it became derailed on the approach to Platform 1 at London Bridge, where it could be clearly seen by all City travellers as they left the station and crossed Tooley Street, immediately below the engine. At this time Nos. 35028-30 had been allocated to Dover for service on the heavy 'Night Ferry' services. No. 35029 was not rerailed until the early hours of the following day and the incident therefore caused some degree of chaos in the evening rush-hour traffic. It was more usual for these engines to work in and out of Victoria. No. 35029 is seen with its nameplates partially covered, although the 'Merchant Navy Class' legend can be seen. The locomotive was not formally named until March 1 1951, at a ceremony held at Southampton Docks, when Directors of the Shipping Company unveiled the *Ellerman Lines* nameplates. The 'Merchant Navies' were all extensively rebuilt in BR days to conform more with the BR Standard engines, losing their 'air-smoothed' plating in the process. No. 35029 was one of the last examples to be rebuilt, in 1959, and is currently well-known as a sectionalised exhibit at the National Railway Museum, York.

were numbered 1-22; in fact there was no Platform 5, since this was a through line not served by any platform. The extension towards Charing Cross involved the erection of two large and rather ugly girder bridges, the second of which crossed Borough High Street at the foot of the road bridge over the River Thames. The station, although not top of the league for the number of passengers carried, is probably the busiest London station on the basis of the number of trains, either terminating or running through to Charing Cross or Cannon Street. For example, in 1967 the three stations handled 1,635 trains and more than 350,000 passengers each weekday.

Right: This mishap outside London Bridge, near Spa Road, Bermondsey, on January 22 1947, is included if only to show the extent of the 11 adjoining tracks here. This rear end collision occurred in dense fog when LBSCR Class I3 4-4-2T No. 2028 collided with the rear of the 10.6am London Bridge-Crystal Palace electric train. No. 2028 was working the empty coaches of an arrival from Tunbridge Wells West to the sidings at New Cross Gate. These tank engines were among the first express engines of their day to demonstrate the efficiency of superheated steam. When new in 1909, No. 23 (later SR 2023) worked the 'Sunny South Special' on alternate days between Brighton and Rugby with LNWR 'Precursor' Class 4-4-0 No. 7 *Titan*, then unsuperheated. The tank engine ran the 90 miles between East Croydon and Rugby without taking water. The result of the trials was conclusive: the 4-4-2T burned 27.4 lbs of coal and consumed 22.4 gallons of water per mile, the altogether less-impressive figures for the LNWR locomotive were 41.2lbs of coal and 36.6 gallons respectively.

THE West End extension of the SER inevitably involved the demolition of much property, the most important of which involved cutting off a small corner of the site of St. Thomas' Hospital, which demanded £750,000 compensation to rebuild the entire hospital on a new site. In the event, this matter went to arbitration and £296,000 was awarded to the hospital which met substantially more than half the cost of building the new hospital on the Embankment site. Work on the railway extension began in 1860 and the station was opened four years later. The original trussed arch roof (see page 15) was less long-lived than the similar structure at Cannon Street. A programme of roof maintenance commenced at Charing Cross in June 1905 and was still in progress six months later when, with little warning, a large part collapsed on December 5. It was remarkable that none of the workmen were killed, but three passengers lost their lives, as did three workmen engaged in restoring the adjacent Avenue Theatre. A manufacturing flaw in a wrought iron tie-rod, which became progressively weakened, was the cause. The station was closed until the remaining roof could be dismantled and Charing Cross was not reopened until March 19 1906. Following this

CHARING CROSS

disaster it was decided to renew the buildings, a programme that continued until 1913, six years after the completion of the new roof. Charing Cross had been the terminus for SECR continental boat train traffic before the First World War, but in 1920 this was concentrated at Victoria, which was more spacious. The SER main line could be reached by means of the new connections installed between Bickley and Orpington in 1902. Electrification of suburban lines commenced in 1926 and within four years the number of passengers using the terminus had increased by 22,500, to 71,200, a remarkable figure for a modest six-platform station. This happy state of affairs continued for many years but in recent years business has declined at this terminus, due to such factors as increasing numbers of commuters using private cars, and the escalating price of office space in Central London prompting businesses to look elsewhere for their property. In the Second World War, because of its proximity to the seat of government, Charing Cross was severely damaged in air raids, notably in 1940, 1941 and 1944,

when train services suffered interruption. Main line services remained in the charge of steam traction until 1957-1958, when the Hastings service was dieselised, and in 1961 remaining Kent Coast services were electrified. A limiting factor at Charing Cross was that only Platform 6, the westward platform, could accommodate 12-coach trains for the peak-hour business services. Suburban platforms had been lengthened to take ten-car trains from 1954. Full electrification was eventually completed with the extension of the third rail system to Hastings in 1986.

Facing page, lower: An interesting and atmospheric view of the Charing Cross signal box, which was in a prominent position over the running lines, at the end of the Thames Bridge. The box and its interesting array of signals are pictured in September 1919. The photograph with its total absence of trains was probably taken in 1919 to record the effects of a nine-day strike by the National Union of Railwaymen, joined by the Associated Society of Locomotive Engineers and Firemen, although the latter Union had no cause for grievance in this instance. This was later to cause much bitterness between the unions, when the ASLEF strike took place in 1955 and the NUR did not support it.

Left: Charing Cross following the construction of the new roof in 1907. In this picture, workmen are still engaged on roof replacement work and the letters 'SECR', with the Managing Committee's coat-of-arms had yet to be fitted on the fascia board immediately behind the bracket signal. The disc headcode on the Class H 0-4-4T on the left indicates a Charing Cross-Cannon Street train; it may be a main line departure, which in pre-war days also-called at Cannon Street, where a main line locomotive took charge. The other Class H tank engine is presumably on a local service; its headcode has not yet been displayed. Note the bowler - hatted ganger in the foreground. Coupled to the 'H' class engine on the right, and also in the centre of the scene can be seen examples of later-built SECR guards vans, as indicated by the side look-outs provided at each end. Once again, general detail of interest to the modeller includes the constructional details of the wooden platforms and their fixtures.

Above: A January 1924 view of a reboil-ered Stirling Class B1 4-4-0 at Charing Cross, in charge of a Mid Kent Line train. The train is standing in Platform 3 and part of the SECR lettering and coat-of-arms on the roof fascia board are just visible at the top left corner of the picture.

Right: Waiting at the ticket barrier at Charing Cross in January 1924 are a porter on the left and a rather smarter ticket collector on the right. The train at the platform has been worked in by one of the excellent rebuilt Class E1 4-4-0s. Note the SECR ticket machine, from which Edmondson-style platform tickets could be obtained for 1d. Companies dif-fered considerably in their approach to public signs. Here, the SECR says 'All season tickets to be shown.' The GWR generally preferred the more archaic spelling 'shewn.' Note that Pears pro-claimed their product as 'The Soap of Kings' and the 'King of Soaps.' Pear's soap is still with us today - but whatever happened to Foster Clark's soups?

Below: This October 1929 picture shows Class L 4-4-0 No. 760, at the head of brand new Hastings line set No. 478, which presumably was brought to Charing Cross for inspection, for the headcode indicates that the train is bound for the sidings, possibly Blackheath. Wainwright's last design for the SECR was the 'L' Class 4-4-0, but the engines were not built before his retirement in November 1913, and Surtees, the Chief Draughtsman at Ashford, took the opportunity to introduce some refinements. Delivery was required for the 1914 summer service, as the SECR was suffering from a chronic shortage of serviceable engines at that time. Since no UK manufacturer would commit themselves to such a delivery date, it was agreed that the first ten examples (Nos 772-781) would be built by Borsig, of Berlin. In the event they all arrived by June 1914, by which time R.E.L. Maunsell was in charge. Twelve engines ordered simultaneously at a higher price from Beyer Peacock, of Manchester, were not all received until three months later, by which time war had broken out. The 'Germans,' as they were often known, were something of a bargain - particularly as payment could not be finalised until 1920.

Left: Severe damage to the station sustained in a daylight air raid in October 1940. An ARP Warden surveys the shattered scene. The open train doors show that the inscription '1' or '3', according to class of travel, was marked on the inside as well as the outside of the doors; first class travel in the suburban area was abolished the following year. Hitler's intensive bombing of London in 1940 and 1941, which became known as 'The Blitz', placed much strain on the city: for example, London was bombed every night from September 7 to November 2, and regular air raids continued until May of the following year. Other cities were also attacked and Coventry in particular was devastated. During 57 raids, more than 13,500 tons of bombs fell on London, and it is awesome to note that as the war progressed the scale of bombing escalated rapidly. Three years later, the RAF delivered 1,600 tons of bombs *per night* on German targets. More than 15,000 Londoners died during the Blitz and such was the course of the war that until September 1941 the enemy had killed more civilians than soldiers, sailors and airmen combined. The capital's railways suffered other major disruption during the war, such as in 1944, when a V1 'flying bomb' scored an unlucky direct hit on Hungerford Bridge, over the Thames, temporarily closing the up and down local lines.

CANNON STREET

**Above: A May 1922 view at Cannon Street;
on the left, a reboilered Stirling 'Q1' 0-4-4T
No. 419 is approaching with a Mid Kent line
train, whilst on the right, 1914-built Class L
4-4-0 No. 777 (one of the German-built
series, see page 45) passes with a main line
train from Dover and Folkestone, including
a Pullman Car in its formation. On the
SECR, Pullman cars were painted in a dark
red lake livery. At the western side of the
bridge, a Class H 0-4-4T waits in readiness
to haul empty stock out of the station. The
engine partly concealed by steam, awaiting
signals in front of the Pullman car, is a
reboilered Stirling 4-4-0, in charge of a train
from Purley. The picture illustrates clearly
the intricacy and complexity of the track
layouts that characterised the approaches to
major stations. No class L 4-4-0s survived
the cutters torch, but happily, an example of
the 'H' class 0-4-4T, No. 263 (built 1905), can
still be seen on the Bluebell Railway.**

COMPARATIVELY little has been
written about this City terminus,
the opening of which took place in
1866, two years after the SER West
End extension to Charing Cross
commenced operation. Both stations had impressive hotels, designed by E.M. Barry, fronting their
splendid train sheds. Unlike the
Charing Cross Hotel, the Cannon
Street Terminus Hotel was less
successful and was leased for
offices in 1931, to be demolished in
BR days, a fate shared by the train
shed roof. Today, only the restored
supporting columns remain as a
reminder of past glories.

Cannon Street's proximity to Fleet
Street and the Press agencies
ensured a degree of photographic
coverage which otherwise might not
have been considered necessary or
newsworthy. Suburban travel into
Cannon Street before electrification
must indeed have been a miserable
business. Many trains were hauled

by elderly Stirling engines hauling
equally old close-coupled four-
wheeled carriages. The SER owned
only two sets of close-coupled bogie
carriages, for outer suburban work;
they were gas lit vehicles built in
1880, and, like the non-bogie
coaches, were soon discarded by
the SR after then Grouping. Six of
the bogie coaches met a spectacular
end in the 1928 film *The Wrecker*.
Punctuality at Cannon Street was
abysmal and the early 1926 electrification must have been greatly welcomed, even though most of the
new EMUs were produced by converting four wheeled coaches dating
from the 1890s. The carriage bodies
were used in pairs, on a single bogie
underframe.

The complicated track layout at
Cannon Street was controlled by a
large 243-lever signal box, spanning
eight tracks at the end of the station
platforms. The pre-war practice of
running main line trains into and

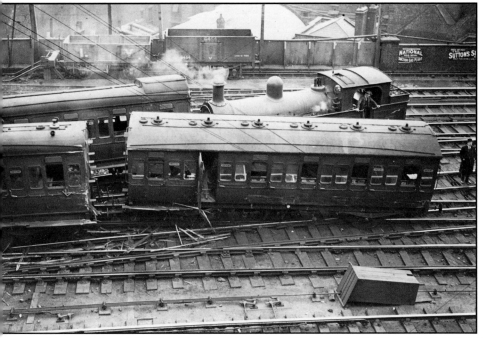

Left: In the height of the evening rush hour on May 13 1925, the driver of rebuilt Stirling Class Q1 0-4-4T No. A 415 overran a danger signal when working the 4.37pm North Kent line train from Erith and collided with another Q1 0-4-4T, No. A76, on the 4.58pm from Bromley North at a point where the up lines converged. As shown here, the rear two coaches of the departing 5.24 pm to Ash, near Aldershot, in turn collided with the derailed coaches. The six-compartment carriage in the centre of the view is an elderly six-wheeled gas-lit coach, of 1880s vintage. There is a mystery here, since the coach next to 0-4-4T No. A76 is in Southern Railway livery and carries the number 761; yet there is no record of any such number for any SECR coach in the SR series. SECR No. 761 is listed as a composite brake coach but is said not to have had a 'birdcage' guards look-out, a claim clearly refuted by this picture. By the following year it is likely that No. 761 was converted into electric stock. Note the footplateman in the engine's cab: he may well be worrying about the forthcoming inquiry into the incident!

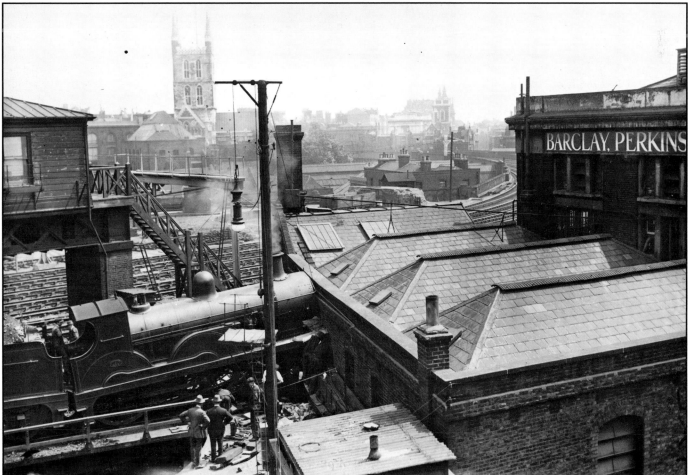

Above: "SR engine runs into brewery" reads the original caption for this August 1926 scene. In fact, reboilered Stirling Class B1 4-4-0 No. A454 has overrun the turntable in the Cannon Street engine sidings. Note the sharp curve of the line to Borough Market Junction and London Bridge; the equally sharp spur joining the line to Charing Cross is concealed by Barclay Perkins brewery. Cannon Street No. 2 signalbox above the engine had 87 levers. Of interest in this picture is that on the far side of the line, above the last roof section of the brewery to the right of the tall chimney, is a wagon seemingly engaged in the removal of rubble from the demolished Cannon Street engine shed, while beyond the suspended lamp (above the derailed engine) can be seen the turntable pit of the old shed.

out of Charing Cross, to or from Cannon Street, via Metropolitan Junction, had been discontinued by the mid-1920s, enabling rationalisation of the old layout. First, the new layout, to a length of 1,000ft, was laid out in the Engineers Yard at New Cross Gate. Every part was then numbered and Cannon Street was closed from 3pm on Saturday June 5 to 4am Monday June 28 1926, to enable the new track layout to be delivered in sections. The old signal box was also demolished and replaced by a new structure with all-electric operation of the newly-installed colour light signalling. The cramped engine shed on the Borough Market Junction side of the bridge was closed and the site used for a sub-station. The turntable and locomotive sidings on the western side remained. At this time, only Platforms 1-5 could be used for electric trains, platforms 6-8 retaining steam workings only for longer distance trains. At the same time, the station concourse was also greatly improved. There was a marked improvement in punctuality, doubtless much appreciated by the 56,000 weekday commuters. Passenger traffic doubled following electrification, although in recent years Cannon Street has been closed in the evenings and at week-ends.

Right, top: With gangers at work in the foreground on June 8, during the alterations of 1926, the base of the old overhead signal box is visible, with the new signalbox just in view behind the right-hand ganger.

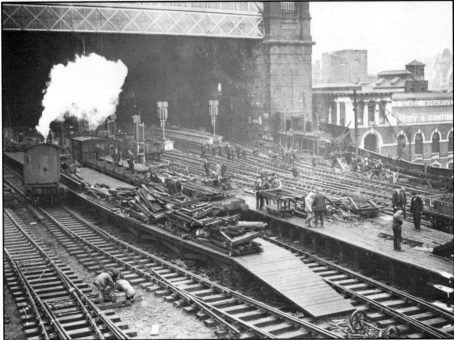

Right, centre: Also taken on June 8, from the steps of the old signal box, this view gives an indication of the scale of the operation. Note that the colour light signals are already in position, while the coal stage and water column near Platform 1 were awaiting removal. The scrap metal on the platform in the foreground came from the dismantling of the old signal box.

Right, lower: This distant view of the station during the 1926 remodelling shows the old signal box to have been completely demolished whilst the new paint of its replacement stands out just off the platform on the left. The impressive overall roof and towers can be seen to advantage, built to the design of J.W. Hawkshaw. Platform awnings were provided following removal of the glass for safety reasons during the Second World War. In 1958-9 the old roof was dismantled leaving only the two towers, which were completely cleaned and restored in 1985.

Left On January 3 1938, 'King Arthur' Class 4-4-0 No. 800 *Sir Meleaus de Lile,* whilst running light, came into side-long collision with the rear carriage of a down steam-worked empty stock train, presumably involving the narrow-width Hastings line carriage seen in the foreground. Cannon Street was closed during clearance operations, trains being diverted to either Charing Cross or London Bridge. The Bricklayers Arms breakdown train is in attendance, in the charge of a Wainwright Class C 0-6-0. The breakdown train consists of three LCDR bogie composite coaches built 1897-8 for boat train service. This is interesting, for the LCDR did not own many bogie carriages. The photographer is presumably standing on the roof of the electrical sub-station occupying the site of the old engine shed. The train immediately in the foreground is a down electric train, which although only partially visible, would probably have comprised a three-coach motor set, a two-coach trailer set and a three coach motor set. The breakdown crane appears to be in the charge of an LBSCR Class C2X 0-6-0. The 'King Arthur' would have worked an up peak-hour express into Charing Cross and arrived at Cannon Street via the connecting spur, in order to turn for its return journey. It carries an Ashford duty number on the headcode disc.

Above: An undated but nevertheless remarkable aerial view of Cannon Street station, in the pre-war period, as the roof is intact and there is no bomb damage evident. Note the former hotel building, by then used as offices, in front of the train shed. Tower Bridge is also prominent, and the Tower of London is dimly visible in the distance. In the streets in the immediate foreground can be seen at least two open-top double deck buses.

HOLBORN VIADUCT, LUDGATE HILL & BLACKFRIARS.

Above: Entitled 'track men at work' this June 5 1932 photograph gives a rare glimpse of the tiny engine shed at Holborn Viaduct, latterly used as a permanent way depot. It was demolished during the war when the platform was extended. The nearest engine servicing depot was at Ewer Street, Southwark, adjacent to the Charing Cross-London Bridge line. This could be used equally by engines from Cannon Street, Charing Cross or Holborn Viaduct. The picture clearly shows the operation of the screw clamp used by permanent way men to ensure rail joints were properly aligned.

Above: The first post war enthusiasts railtour was organised jointly by the Stephenson Locomotive Society and the Southern Counties Touring Society. Starting from Kensington and finishing at Victoria it traversed some lines not normally open to passenger traffic; indeed one spur, that from Beckenham Junction to Norwood Junction has since been lifted. Its first stop was at Ludgate Hill, closed in 1929 when the Wimbledon-service was electrified. On April 15 1950 it was surprising to find the platforms of the old station still in such good condition. Even the posters still remained, one of them extolling the virtues of the 'Sunny South Express', although this travelled from north to south via the West London Line. The only passenger trains to traverse Ludgate Hill and the Metropolitan widened lines since closure in 1916 would have been an occasional troop train. Wainwright Class C 0-6-0 No. 31716, which provided motive power throughout, runs round the train at Ludgate Hill. One of the authors was a passenger on this train, but is not amongst those pictured here!

THE LCDR reached the south end of Blackfriars Bridge in 1864, the site later being used for Southwark Goods Depot. The following year the railway was extended to Ludgate Hill and a year later a connection was installed to join with the Metropolitan Railway at Faringdon; this line was initially intended to convey coal and freight from the northern railway companies - the GNR and MR. An intermediate station was provided at Snow Hill in 1874 for passenger traffic, and soon an impressive train service was running between North and South London. Latterly known as Holborn Viaduct Low Level, this station closed in 1916, through passenger services ceasing at the same time, and, with the spread of smokeless zones under the Clean Air Act leading to a decline in the demand for coal, the last coal train ran in 1969, after which the tracks were lifted. It is these tracks which were reinstated in 1987 for the Thames Link service, due to commence in 1988. Ludgate Hill was used for through trains from the LSWR, initially from Twickenham, via Richmond, Hammersmith and Shepherds Bush, latterly only from Wimbledon, some taking the now-closed loop line via Merton Abbey, but the station closed altogether in 1929. Because of the SECR's shortage of carriage sidings in the immediate London area, it was used until the end of steam running for empty stock trains, engines running round their trains in readiness to work either to Cannon Street or Charing Cross as main line platforms became vacant. The LCDR City line had never had its underbridges strengthened, unlike the line to Victoria in early SR days, hence the largest engines permitted were the rebuilt Class D1 and E1 4-4-0s.

Ludgate Hill soon proved to be inadequate for the increasing traffic and a new six-platform station at Holborn Viaduct was opened in

1874. This proved more than adequate and the western side of the station became an important parcels depot, remembered in the 1930s for exclusively horse-drawn road vehicles. This traffic survived in BR days and the rebuilt 4-4-0s could still be seen until electrification of SECR main lines in 1961. Steam passenger trains had ceased on electrification of the lines to Maidstone and Gillingham in 1939. The station was severely damaged by enemy action and has been totally rebuilt since the last war.

In 1886, by means of a new bridge over the Thames, a new station was opened at St. Pauls, having three terminal platforms and two through lines to Holborn Viaduct. There were seven tracks across the new (and more elegant) bridge built to serve this station: the original girder bridge across the Thames was demolished in 1985, thus removing something of an eyesore. Ludgate Hill Station has also been long demolished and, for a few years before the laying of the Thames Link lines, the site was used for off-peak EMU stabling. St Pauls was especially notable in that it dis-

Above: The Inspector looks happy to see this unusual train on its way again, from Ludgate Hill station. To his left can be seen the obligatory (in those days) wheeltapper with his hammer, and behind the other railwaymen can be seen part of Blackfriars station. Also beyond the engine tender can be seen the unsightly girder bridge, since demolished.

played the names of places having home or continental connections with the LCDR. Thus, Baden Baden and Beckenham appeared as did Rome and Ramsgate! Even the booking office counter carried a reminder, in both English and French, to examine your change! St

Pauls was renamed Blackfriars in 1937 to coincide with the adjacent District Line station and it was substantially rebuilt in the 1970s. Trains now terminate here in the evenings, when Holborn Viaduct is closed, and both stations are usually closed at week-ends.

Above: A glimpse of Holborn Viaduct station on April 27 1948, showing a new Bulleid '4 SUB' EMU set with its British Railways lettering. When this type was introduced after the war, they originally carried the name 'Southern' in this position, but very soon reverted to showing the unit number only. They looked attractive in their malachite green livery and one survivor remains for use at special events - Unit No.4732, repainted in the once-familiar green. The 83 headcode indicates a Holborn Viaduct-Sevenoaks train, a service due to be partly taken over (as this book went to press) by the Thames Link units, outside peak hours. The 'S' regional prefix to the unit number was also subsequently dropped. At right is one of the Wainwright Class H 0-4-4Ts, once familiar at Holborn Viaduct, shunting parcels vans.

Chapter 3: New Works

STATIONS & CIVIL ENGINEERING

THE Southern Railway was always a very 'go-ahead' company, and under its dynamic management progress was rapid. Although the SR was committed to a policy of suburban electrification with a time-interval service, it did not neglect improvements to its steam-operated lines. Not only were many stations rebuilt, examples being Wimbledon, Kingston, Richmond, Surbiton, Dover, Ramsgate and Hastings, but several engine sheds were also substantially modernised, including Exmouth Junction and also Brick-

layers Arms, which was sorely in need of improvement..

Improvements were carried out at other London depots, notably Stewarts Lane, the former LCDR Longhedge shed, later to take over the major part of the allocation of the closed LBSCR shed at Battersea Park. A new coal stage was built at nearby Nine Elms, while completely new sheds were opened in the 1930s at Hither Green and Norwood Junction. The LSWR had opened a concrete works at Exmouth Junction in 1913 and under the SR it built up

a range of many standard parts for new stations, or for the extension or rebuilding of existing stations. The first new lines to be opened were two previously-authorised light railways, the Totton Hythe and Fawley Railway and the North Devon & Cornwall Junction Light Railway. This was a grandiose title indeed for a single line connecting Torrington with Halwill Junction, on the North Cornwall line, at a point where the branch to Bude diverged. Densely overgrown, Halwill Junction survives (at the time of

Above: The North Devon & Cornwall Junction Light Railway was opened in July 1925, part of its tracks replacing the previous 3ft gauge Torrington & Marland Railway. Passenger traffic from the outset was disappointing, the ball clay conveyed by the former industrial line comprising the staple traffic. It is of interest to note that the indefatigable supporter of light railways, Colonel Holman F. Stephens, was the Consulting Engineer for this line. The previous narrow gauge industrial line had used a former horse-drawn London tramcar body, carried on railway wheels, to carry its workmen, and a scaled-down replica of this remarkable coach is in service today on the narrow gauge Launceston Steam Railway, which covers a small portion of the former LSWR North Cornwall

line. Intermediate stations on the NDCJLR were sparsely equipped, except at Hatherleigh, and even this was not especially distinctive. Because of its light railway status, limited axle loading was required for the branch, early motive power comprising 1884-vintage Adams 4-4-0s of Class 0460, transferred to the duplicate list. SR No. E 0462 is pictured here at Hatherleigh on July 28 1925, in charge of the inaugural train. Even the LSWR rolling stock looks archaic! Perhaps the second high-roof coach was for the railway officers forming the majority of the passengers present. These 4-4-0s were soon replaced by LBSCR Stroudley Class E1 0-6-0Ts, rebuilt at Brighton Works with an additional trailing axle to support an enlarged bunker, thereby forming the Class E1/R 0-6-2Ts.

Above: The rebuilt station at Exmouth in September 1925, with Adams Class O2 0-4-4T No. E 192 in charge of a local train to Exeter. Note at right the concrete slabs from Exmouth Junction concrete works. Exmouth Junction, where the line left the main line between Waterloo and Exeter, was actually some nine miles from Exmouth. The Exmouth branch, with its busy service to Exeter, and also the branch to Barnstaple, were the only SR branches in Devon to escape the Beeching axe, which closed all other branches and even the former LSWR main line to Plymouth, beyond Meldon Quarry, near Okehampton, principal source of ballast to the SR. Further west, only the line from Plymouth, through Bere Ferrers, to Gunnislake survives and this has been partly diverted in the Devonport area over former GWR lines. The lengthy platform at Exmouth was to accommodate the one-time through coaches to and from Waterloo.

going to press) as something of a ghost station.

The most important undertaking was the rationalisation of the lines in Thanet. The previous rivals, the LCDR and SER each had stations on different lines serving Margate and Ramsgate. The SER line between Ramsgate Town and Margate Sands was abandoned as was the LCDR Ramsgate Harbour line and a new line made an end-on connection at a new Ramsgate station on the outskirts of the town, where a new engine shed was built, replacing two previous depots. Margate station, rebuilt in connection with the scheme, was fully operational in July 1926. A similar scheme took place nearby at Dover, where the former Harbour station was closed in 1927, Priory station being rebuilt and a new engine shed opened. New loop lines were also opened at Lewisham in 1929 partly making use of the old LCDR. Greenwich Park branch, closed in 1917, but intended primarily to give access to the important sidings at Hither Green for cross-London freight trains to and from the lines of other companies. In the same year, a new line was opened between

Left: An Officers Inspection Special toured the new arrangements for the lines in Thanet, brought about by the concentration of traffic on a single through line, joining the former SER and LCDR routes by means of a new connecting line, with new stations, at Ramsgate and Dumpton Park to the east. On July 3 1926, railway managers alight from their Pullman Cars to inspect the construction of the new Dumpton Park station. Note that on ex-SECR lines at this time the Pullmans still carried an all-lake livery. The train is hauled either by a Class D1 or an E1 4-4-0, a lightweight load for such an engine. The event must have been advertised in advance judging by the onlookers. The new lines were opened on July 19 1926. The original Topical Press captions records that this was the first train to call at the station and that the new railway had cost £500,000 to construct.

Above: Cutting out a traffic bottleneck at Blackwater, on the SECR line between Guildford and Reading, August 20 1930. In this very attractive scene, a road overbridge is being constructed to replace the level crossing. Note that the contractor then relied upon horse drawn transport, while on the road Morris and Austin cars predominate, accompanied by a Maudslay coach, on its way to Bournemouth. The train engine is Maunsell Class 2-6-0 No. A801, then recently rebuilt from a 'River' Class 2-6-4T. Maunsell 2-6-0s could be seen throughout the SR system from west to east and were very common on the Redhill-Guildford-Reading line, only parts of which are electrified, the Reading-Tonbridge service now being operated by DMUs from Western Region.

Above: Construction of the new station at Tinsley Green, for Gatwick Airport, on September 27 1935. The airport had started life as little more than a flying field for the Surrey Aero Club in 1930 but major developments were planned by the pioneers of British Airways Ltd (no connection with the present British Airways) who had previously flown from a former military airfield at Heston. Although the station looked far from complete, it was in fact opened to traffic three days later (September 30) no doubt in very unfinished condition. Under the title 'A new luxury aerodrome for London' the original caption claimed that although 25 miles from London, passengers would be in the capital within half an hour. In fact, it was nearer 27 miles and the trains took 42 minutes; however the caption writer may have had the gift of second sight, for the present Gatwick Express service takes 30 minutes, but only following substantial route improvements. A Maunsell Class U1 2-6-0 is running down light as the up 'Brighton Belle' Pullman train passes. The station was renamed Gatwick Airport on June 1 1936, five days before the Airport's formal opening.

Below: Gatwick Airport station in far more complete condition, seen in May 1936, with the concrete air terminal (nowadays referred to as the 'Beehive') which surpassed any previous buildings on British airports. An underground subway connected the terminal to the station. The airport was closed from 1956 to 1958 to allow its total reconstruction, and the 'Beehive' is now isolated from the airport, although still intact. As part of the modernisation programme, this first Gatwick Airport station was closed and a new station opened in May 1958, on the site of the former LBSCR Gatwick Racecourse station.

Left: Among the SR's station renewal work was the rebuilding of Exeter Central (opened formally in July 1933) pictured here on July 9 1936. Fortunately, in deference to a splendid city, the SR did not erect one of its concrete buildings to which it was so partial. The former LSWR Queen Street station on this site had an overall roof, removed during the rebuilding. The outside 'wings', above the shops, were used as railway offices.

Wimbledon and Sutton, electrified from the outset, to forestall the Underground group extending beyond Morden.

A new line from Motspur Park to Chessington South was opened by 1939, but the war and Green Belt legislation prevented it reaching its intended ultimate destination of Leatherhead. On a wider scale, electrification was proceeding apace, as was the extension of Southampton Docks, both subjects dealt with separately in this book.

Left: With the vast extension works at Southampton Docks carried out by the SR, it was decided to rebuild the main line station. At the same time, the formation west of the station was widened to Millbrook, east of which two tracks entered the Docks, making an alternative entry to the Southampton Terminus access. Trains could be reversed by entering the Docks via the Terminus and leaving via Millbrook, or vice versa. Millbrook is now the site of an important container terminal so the widened lines are much-needed. When this photograph was taken, on January 30 1934, the works were far from complete and a new road bridge was being built over the tracks. The down train passing through is being hauled by a rebuilt Drummond Class 700 0-6-0, a design dating from 1897. Like some of Drummond's 4-4-0s, this class was rebuilt with superheated boilers in the 1920s.

Right & below: Considerable work was carried out in 1936 in connection with the installation of colour light signalling, to improve the approach to Waterloo station, enabling a reduction in headway times between trains from four to two minutes. New power signal boxes were provided at Waterloo, Surbiton and Hampton Court Junction, but a most dramatic development was the rearrangement of tracks at Wimbledon. Previously, the up and down local lines were situated either side of the main lines, thereby causing frequent conflicting movements across the main line near the terminus. The construction of a flyover on the London side of Wimbledon station eliminated this and aligned the main and local lines side-by-side. The new arrangement came into use on May 17 1936, the new Waterloo signal box becoming operational the following October. These pictures illustrate construction of the Wimbledon flyover.

Above: Work in progress at Wimbledon, February 10 1936, looking towards London. In the distant left is the Durnsford Road electric depot and power station. To cope with subsequent electrification extensions, this depot was considerably extended and is now known as Wimbledon Park. The flyover when complete was to take London-bound local services, bringing them on to the former down main line on the right, on which an EMU converted from LSWR steam stock is seen on a Hampton Court train. On the up local line is one of the original LSWR 'bullet-nose' EMUs.

Left: The London end of the flyover, with an ex-works type 2-NOL EMU Set No 1863 occupying the up local line in the foreground, whilst in the background is another of the former LSWR 'bullet-nose' units.

Left: The new SR branch from Motspur Park to Malden Manor and Tolworth was opened on May 29 1938, following this May 25 visit of representatives of the Boroughs of Malden and Surbiton. The station was of reinforced concrete, much-used by the SR in stations built or rebuilt in the London area, and the pillarless platform roofs are said to have been admired. During excavations for the station site, rocks 27ft below the surface were found to be embedded with fossil shells which British Museum experts estimated to be 20 million years old. The new line was intended to serve the rapidly growing residential area south of the Kingston by-pass. The line was extended from Tolworth to Chessington South on May 28 1939.

ELECTRIFICATION

Above: Although of indifferent quality, this is an interesting 1909 view of one of the original LBSCR three-coach South London Line sets (of which there were eight) entering Wandsworth Road station, en route to Victoria. As introduced, these units were painted, as shown here, in a smart umber and cream livery. Although the scheme was regarded as successful it soon became clear that the provision of an entire First Class trailer coach was not required, especially in off-peak periods, and these were withdrawn and adapted for main line steam use. The South London units subsequently consisted of one motor coach, accompanied by a driving trailer coach converted from steam suburban stock. The other mistake not repeated was in the 9ft 3in width of these coaches, which prevented their working through Crystal Palace Tunnel, hence their availability was restricted. They were converted to two car units in BR days, eight sets of the wide coaches working the South London Line (as third rail sets) until the mid 1950s. The original First Class coaches were also converted into four two-coach sets and used on the Wimbledon-West Croydon service, until 1954.

THE LBSCR 'ELEVATED ELECTRIC' SYSTEM

THE LBSCR obtained powers to electrify the whole of its system as early as 1903, and having looked at various systems used on the continent of Europe, it decided as an initial experiment to convert the South London Line between London Bridge, Peckham Rye and Victoria, which was losing traffic to the newly-electrified trams. The Company's Consulting Engineer recommended the use of high-tension single phase alternating current at 6,700 volts, supplied from overhead wires, in the belief that it would be suitable not only for the suburban system but also for later main line extensions to the South Coast. In 1906, Allgemeine Elektricitats Gesellschaft, of Berlin, was awarded the contract for the electrical equipment, although switchgear and cabling contracts were sub-let to British firms. In 1902, the South London Line had carried eight million passengers annually but by 1909 this number had been halved; this trend was reversed in the first year of electric working which commenced in December 1909. The main power station was situated at Deptford and an electric stock carriage shed and maintenance depot was built at Peckham Rye. These trains provided only First and Third Class accommodation, the LBSCR abandoning Second Class travel, other than on boat trains, in 1912, this provision on suburban trains having ceased in 1911. The system was extensively advertised as the

'Elevated Electric' and in 1911-12 the lines between Victoria and London Bridge to Crystal Palace were electrified.

Further extensions of the LBSCR system were halted in 1914 on the outbreak of war since it was no longer possible to obtain equipment from the German suppliers. Nevertheless work was carried out in erection of overhead masts from Balham Junction to West Croydon and Tulse Hill to Streatham Common. Work on extensions to Coulsdon and Sutton was recom- menced in 1922 but was not com- plete at the time of the 1923 Grouping. By this time, the LSWR had completed the electrification of its inner suburban lines on the 600 volt direct current third rail system and since its electrified mileage was considerably in excess of that of the LBSCR it was decided to continue that part of the overhead electrifica- tion still in hand, but at the earliest opportunity, bearing in mind the urgency of electrifying SECR subur- ban lines, the overhead system would be replaced by third rail.

Below: The final extension to the LBSCR's 'Elevated Electric' system occurred on April 1 1925, on the Balham-Coulsdon North and Sutton (via Selhurst) lines. These trains were entirely different from those used pre- viously, and featured a centrally placed powered motor coach, with a pair of passen- ger coaches front and rear, including driving trailers, as illustrated here. This picture was taken on March 31 1925 at Carshalton Beeches, during an officers inspection visit - note all the bowler hats on the platform, indicating officialdom at large! The station looks barely complete. Following the aban- donment of the overhead system, these units were converted for third rail operation.

Right: Another view at Carshalton Beeches on March 31 1925, the day before public services over the newly-electrified route commenced. At peak times, two of the five-car sets were coupled and operated` in multiple. The powered car is clearly seen in the middle of the train: following the full adop- tion of the third rail system in preference to the overhead system, the 21 powered motor coaches were converted to become goods brake vans, at Eastleigh. The remaining coaches were converted for third rail use.

LSWR ELECTRIFICATION

THE LSWR had electric trains running over some of its tracks as early as 1905, when the District Railway between Richmond and Hammersmith, and from Putney Bridge to Wimbledon, had been energised. In 1912, there was a rumour that the Central London Railway (later to become part of the Underground system) was seeking powers to extend to Richmond. This action, never pursued, stimulated the LSWR to plan its suburban electrification. It already had a short stretch of electrified line in the 1898 Waterloo & City Railway, familiarly known as 'The Drain', which had the distinction of being London's second oldest tube line and the only underground railway owned and operated by a main line company. The LSWR sought advice from the USA and chose the 600 volt dc system, similar to that used on the City line, also a third rail system, but at a lower voltage. As early as 1913, the foundations of the

power station at Wimbledon were being prepared. Other work carried out in connection with electrification included the 1915 provision of a flyover at Hampton Court Junction. The LSWR electric stock consisted of 84 three-car 'bullet-nose' sets, converted from bogie suburban trains, built from 1904. The important feature of electrification was the introduction of a fixed interval train service, an arrangement perpetuated by the SR.

During 1915 and 1916, the LSWR inner suburban layout was electrified with commendable speed and in the first four mainly wartime years of electrification, passenger traffic on these lines increased by 74%. Clearly this showed the way forward for Sir Herbert Walker, the

Above: Adams Class 02 0-4-4T No. 179 shunts coal up to the bunkers above the boiler house at the generating station at Durnsford Road, Wimbledon. The bunkers had a capacity of 1,400 tons of coal. Not all the wagons in this train are destined for the coal bunkers - those at the head of the train are tarpaulin covered. The LBSCR and LSWR power stations survived into early BR days. Constructed of brick, the power house was equipped with 16 Babcock & Wilcox boilers, each with an evaporation rate of 20,000lbs of water per hour. Arranged in two rows with a firing platform between them, the boilers were fired by chain grate stokers, and provided steam at 200psi. Five main turbo-alternators generated three-phase power at 11,000 volts, whilst three auxiliary generating sets were capable of producing continuous current at 220 volts. Continuity of water supply was ensured by the provision of an overhead tank containing 110,000 gallons. Water for condensing came from the neighbouring River Wandle; after passing through condensers, it was returned to the river via a series of cascades, ensuring that it was cooled to within a few degrees of inlet temperature before it rejoined the Wandle.

LSWR's General Manager, who assumed the same post on formation of the Southern Railway in 1923.

Above: A view of the inclined gantry leading up to the coal bunkers, also in February 1915. The gantry was constructed with an open deck for much of its length (see inset) permitting the stockpiling of up to 10,000 tons of coal on the ground, in addition to the 1,400 tons of fuel carried in the hoppers above the boiler room. There had been experience of a miners strike in 1912 and worse was to come in 1919 and 1926, so this extra storage capacity was a useful feature. With a total length of 550ft, the gantry was 19ft wide and comprised a single 50ft steel girder span (immediately outside the building) and 20 ferro-concrete spans of 25ft each. Ashes were drawn out of the boiler house by a vacuum system and stored in the torpedo-shaped hopper at the end of the short siding, where they were discharged into wagons for disposal. The huge chimneys were 230ft tall, with an internal diameter at the top of more than 13ft.

Right: A view inside the bunker house, with a pair of Stephenson Clarke's wagons standing ready to discharge coal.

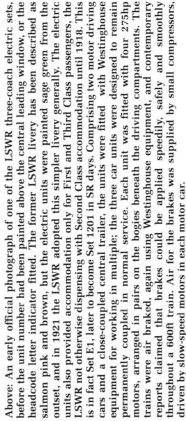

Above: An early official photograph of one of the LSWR three-coach electric sets, before the unit number had been painted above the central leading window, or the headcode letter indicator fitted. The former LSWR livery has been described as salmon pink and brown, but the electric units were painted sage green from the outset, and in 1921 the LSWR adopted this simpler livery generally. The electric units also provided accommodation only for First and Third Class passengers, the LSWR not otherwise dispensing with Second Class accommodation until 1918. This is in fact Set E1, later to become Set 1201 in SR days. Comprising two motor driving cars and a close-coupled central trailer, the units were fitted with Westinghouse equipment for working in multiple; the three car units were designed to remain permanently coupled in normal service. Each unit was fitted with four 275hp motors, arranged in pairs on the bogies beneath the driving compartments. The trains were air braked, again using Westinghouse equipment, and contemporary reports claimed that brakes could be applied speedily, safely and smoothly throughout a 600ft train. Air for the brakes was supplied by small compressors, driven by slow-speed motors in each motor car.

Left: A close-up view of the cast steel current collector shoes fitted on these units, to obtain current from the third rail. The conductor rails were laid 16in from the running rail and with its contact surface 3in above running rail level. Manufactured using special high conductivity steel and weighing 100lbs per yard, the third rail was supported by porcelain insulators. The electrical return was achieved via the running rails, whose fishplated joints were bonded with copper straps. The rails were also cross-bonded at intervals to equalise the return current. The 11,000-volt supply was distributed from Durnsford Road to nine sub-stations, where it was transformed to a continuous voltage of 600 volts DC and fed to the conductor rails. The sub stations were at Waterloo, Clapham Junction, Raynes Park, Hampton Court Junction, Kingston, Sunbury, Twickenham, Isleworth and Barnes.

Above: This front view shows the 'bullet-nose' effect of these units, which was perpetuated on the new EMUs (Nos.1285-1310) built for the 1925 extensions from Raynes Park via Epsom to Dorking, Leatherhead and Effingham Junction, and Claygate to Guildford. Note the brass organ pipe whistle mounted on the right of the drivers window. Each three-car set seated 185 passengers and all 84 sets were originally based at the electric car sheds adjacent to the Durnsford Road power station, as illustrated on page 59. In later years, additional trailers were added and the sets reclassified as '4 SUB' to denote their four car suburban status.

Left: The very spartan cab provided by the LSWR for its suburban motormen. Perhaps the Company was concerned about its drivers falling asleep at the controls in such non-strenuous conditions (compared with a steam locomotive footplate) for not even a seat is provided. The controls were deliberately kept simple, drivers being required only to move the control handle to the full 'on' position when starting away, the Westinghouse relay equipment operating automatically to ensure that the individual motors were 'notched up' according to the varying loads being placed upon them. The designers aim was to equalise the loadings on the two or more motor coaches in a train, and ensure economic use of energy. To eliminate expensive and damaging accidents, the reverser had to be engaged fully in either direction of travel before the motorman could operate the controller, which was also fitted with a 'dead man' system. If the driver allowed the spring-loaded handle to rise from its normal position, the current was cut-off from the motors and the brakes applied: in these circumstances the controller had to be moved to the off position before the brakes could be released. During coasting and braking operations the driver had to move the controller to the off position and keep it depressed to avoid a brake application: second nature today to train drivers, but a novel feature at the time no doubt, to footplatemen more accustomed to regulators and vacuum brakes. Gauges for current consumption and air brake pressure are fitted alongside the front window, together with a handle for working the windscreen wiper.

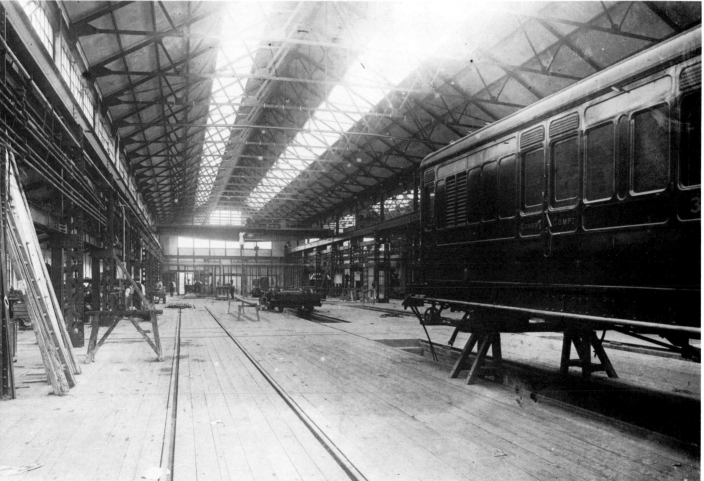

Above: An interesting view of the interior of the EMU maintenance depot at Durnsford Road. In recent years, the carriage sheds have been greatly extended and are now known as Wimbledon Park, a depot with a long history.

LSWR ELECTRIFICATION - A POSTSCRIPT:

THE LSWR's suburban electrification developed traffic to such an extent that from 1919 pairs of trailer coaches, without driving facilities, were converted from steam-hauled stock to reinforce the three-coach units at peak times. The SR continued this practice, which was far from ideal. In the off-peak hours at termini, passengers often had to pass five coaches parked at the buffer stops to board the front three coaches only. It did not pay to 'cut it fine' with your arrival time at the platform! From 1934, the LSWR electric coaches were lengthened, using 62ft underframes, thereby producing the same seating provision as on the other Sections: 56 First Class and 180 Third Class seats. In 1941, First Class travel was abolished

on suburban lines. and from the following year, some sense of order was created by converting the EMUs to four-coach sets and abolishing the trailers. Bulleid had built his first two 4 SUB units in 1941, which seated six-a-side, providing no less than 456 seats but at the cost of comfort. Eight more units of the type were built in 1945, but subsequent 4-SUB sets varied in capacity. Initially, it was thought that First Class travel might be restored and one coach in each unit was of the compartment type, but from 1948 the centre-gangway type coaches were introduced. In 1951, the 4 EPB sets, the present older generation of EMUs, were introduced, these having Westinghouse Electro Pneumatic brakes, hence their designation. Third Class became Second Class in 1956 and is now known as 'Standard Class'.

SR SUBURBAN ELECTRIFICATION

Above: With the building 'boom' that followed successive extensions of the electrified network, the builders or landowners often contributed to the cost of a station to serve new housing developments. This was the case at Hinchley Wood on the Guildford 'New Line' (between Surbiton and Claygate) where the builders subsidised a new station, pictured here on the opening day, October 20 1930. The 'Southern Electric' sign adjacent to the footbridge proclaims: "London in 21 minutes, Frequent fast trains." Whilst workmen on the canopy roof add the finishing touches, one of their colleagues in the foreground is seemingly busy repairing a cycle puncture!

Right: Unit 1281 leads a multiple unit train into Waterloo station, with a service from Hampton Court, on March 19 1938. This was one of the original LSWR 'bullet-nose' sets and the picture depicts the disconcerting habit of commuters opening the doors, alighting and sprinting along the platform before the train has come to a stand.

AFTER the Grouping, since the rolling stock on former LCDR lines was in a parlous state, the lines from Victoria and Holborn Viaduct to Orpington (via the main line) and to Crystal Palace and Shortlands (via the Catford Loop) were given first priority for electrification. The new services started in July 1925. Former SER suburban lines, which were not in much better state, were then tackled, and in 1926 the lines from Cannon Street and Charing Cross (via the Mid Kent line) to Addiscombe and Hayes, the main line to Orpington, the branch from Grove Park to Bromley North and the routes to Dartford were also electrified, a major contribution to the electrified suburban network.

Above: Two up trains stand in Grove Park station on February 27 1926. This was the first day of electric services here, but quite what has happened to the train on the left to require the presence of the officials is not clear, nor is the presence of a flagman to the right of the porters trolley, beneath the tall signal. Both trains are comprised of converted SER coaches. The left hand line, then adapted for through working was previously a bay platform for trains from Bromley North.

Right: There were several routes to Dartford and all were electrified in 1926. Beyond Dartford all services were steam worked at this time, hence the presence of a down steam train to the right of the up electric train, in this June 8 1926 view. The EMU comprises stock converted from SER non bogie coaches. On the platform at right, with the milk churns, is Push-and-Pull set No. 651, doubtless in the charge of a Wainwright Class P 0-6-0T, on the rear. This set consisted of three LCDR four-wheeled coaches, diagrammed to work between Dartford, Gravesend and Port Victoria. It was to be four more years before electrification reached Gravesend.

Left: An up Dartford (via the North Kent line), train leaves Blackheath in June 1926. Thanks to the collaboration of Network South East and local conservationists of the Blackheath Society, this 1849-vintage station is kept in immaculate condition today. The platform canopies have been shortened in recent years and there is no longer a bay platform. This was one of the outer suburban stations that was well provided with carriage sidings, but all have now gone to be replaced by a car park. Note the Coligny-Welch fishtail lamp on the distant signal, soon to be replaced at this time. Reminders of steam hauled passenger services are seen in the shape of the water columns, whilst in the yard is a small hand operated crane of the type once familiar in goods yards throughout the country.

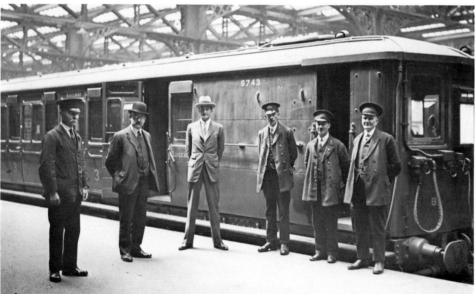

Above: Unit 1295, of the 1925-built Western Section series, is seen entering Guildford on the inaugural day of operations of the newly-electrified 'new line' via Cobham (opened in 1885) in July 1925. Note that although of new construction these coaches were similar in length to the older LSWR electric sets, whose 'bullet-nose' style they perpetuated. This unit appears to have a white or silver roof, but dark grey was the normal colour. A neatly uniformed school party is welcoming the incoming train.

Left, upper: Coach No 8743, of Unit 1766, (converted from LBSCR overhead electric stock) is pictured with a group of railwaymen at Waterloo in July 1930, after returning with the inaugural electric service to Windsor. Note that a larger Guards and luggage compartment was then included than is now considered to be necessary.

EASTERN SECTION (Ex-SECR routes)

Left: A down Orpington train enters Grove Park on Sunday February 28 1926, the first day of the electrified service on this route. Starting the service on a Sunday was a good idea, as it enabled railwaymen to become accustomed to the new timetable and equipment, before the Monday morning rush. The station is little changed today, apart from its colour light signalling and improved station lighting.

Left: On May 1 1934, Unit 1416 (of converted SER stock) stands in the old station at St Mary Cray. The occasion was the opening of the first four miles (from Bickley to St Mary Cray) of the SR's 23-mile electrification extension to Sevenoaks, Kent. In common with many other SECR stations, St Mary Cray had staggered platforms, connected by a footbridge. A new station, with four platform faces, was subsequently provided here in BR days in connection with the 1959 phase of the Kent Coast electrification. The SR's electrification of the 1920s and 1930s was a massive undertaking, and the suburban system in particular was the biggest of its kind in the world in 1930. By that year, the SR suburban network used 1,650 coaches to carry 218 million passengers each year, generating approximately £5 million in fare revenue.

Above: The original Topical Press caption for this picture reads: "By electric trains straight to the Derby Racecourse". Unit 1601, like the train at the adjacent platform, was of converted SER non-bogie stock. The station nameboard is of SECR type, the line not having opened until 1901. It was reached by electrified lines in 1928. Behind the drivers compartment of Unit 1601 is a side-board proclaiming 'London, East Croydon, Purley.' These boards continued in use until the Second World War. The coaches all carried gold leaf letters with designations '1' or '3' according to class of travel. First Class travel was abolished on suburban lines in 1941. The layout at Tattenham Corner, as at the LBSCR's Epsom Downs station, was extensive to permit the working of special trains on race days.

MAIN LINE ELECTRIFICATION

Right: Main line 6-PUL Unit 2019 (later 3019) poses for the photographer, prior to the inauguration of the Brighton electrification, in January 1933. All the Pullman Cars had lady's names, and the vehicle used in Unit 2019 was *Peggy*. These coaches performed yeoman service until eventually replaced in the mid-1960s by 4 BIG and 4-CIG units. Whilst the 'COR' abbreviation may be easily translated to 'corridor', and 'PUL' to 'Pullman car-equipped', the 'BIG' and 'CIG' annotations are less easily explained. In fact, 'IG' was the LBSCR telegraphic code for Brighton! The Pullman cars were stored between 1942 and 1946 and were withdrawn between 1965 and 1968; *Ruth* and *Bertha* survive in preservation.

Above: Following the 1931 introduction of the 'Bournemouth Belle' the name 'Southern Belle (which had been introduced by the LBSCR in 1908 with a new train, although all-Pullman trains had run for some years) seemed no longer entirely appropriate. So, on June 29 1934 the train was renamed the 'Brighton Belle' and here at Victoria we see a typical pose for the photographer, showing the old carriage roof boards giving way to the new. The first down run of the day, at 11 am from Victoria, conveyed a large number of invited guests and the Mayor of Brighton (Councillor Miss Margaret Hardy, MBE) formally renamed the train on arrival at Brighton. The SR had presumably provided her with some statistics, for she announced that the 'Southern Belle' had run nearly one and a quarter million miles since 1908, and carried five million passengers. The 5-BEL sets (all built in 1932) were taken out of service from 1942-6; Unit 3052 was bomb-damaged outside Victoria in 1940 and subsequently stored at Crystal Palace High Level, until repairs could be carried out after the war. Remarkably, all 15 coaches of the three 5 BEL sets survive, some on preserved railways, while others now serve as annexes to public houses. *Audrey* still runs today in the Venice Simplon Orient Express train. The Pullman Car Company having been taken over by the British Transport Commission and the units being due for replacement, the 'Brighton Belle' service ended in 1972.

BY 1935, the whole of the SR suburban system was electrified, but even earlier the Company had decided to electrify the former LBSCR main lines to Brighton and Worthing.

Completion of this scheme meant that the SR was by 1933 operating 359 route miles (978 track miles) of electrified railway, including both suburban and main line routes. The Brighton/Worthing line was electrified in view of its importance in terms of traffic, for at this time nearly 1,750,000 passengers used the route.

The first stage, opened on July 17 1932, was the electrification of the line as far as Three Bridges (via Redhill) for which 33 four-coach lavatory-equipped non-corridor sets were provided. One of these can be seen in front of the Victoria power signal box pictured under construction on page 37. On January 1 1933, the electrification was complete, at an overall cost of nearly £3 million, and for this scheme 23 six-car EMU sets were built, each including a Pullman car as part of the formation. These 6 PUL sets were originally numbered 2001-20 (later renumbered 3001-20) while the

balance of three sets became Nos.3041-3, the distinction being that this group provided more First Class accommodation for the 'City Limited' working between Brighton and London Bridge in peak hours.

In addition, five all-Pullman sets were built, (Nos.3051-3) for the 'Southern Belle' service. These trains attracted much attention, for not only were they the world's first motor Pullman cars, at 62 tons apiece (motor coaches only) the all-steel vehicles were the heaviest coaches yet used on British railways. Each five-car formation consisted of: third class motor Pullman brake, third class Pullman, two first class Pullmans with kitchens and a third class motor Pullman brake. The 249 tons (tare) trains could seat 40 first class and 152 third class passengers.

By 1933, the SR's programme of train construction for its electrification scheme totalled 285 vehicles, including 38 Pullman cars. The Brighton line was the first in the country to obtain power direct from the Central Electricity Board, via three sub-stations at Croydon, Three Bridges and Southwick. Extensive

colour light signalling was also provided on the route, featuring much automatic operation.

In 1935, electrification of the LBSCR line to Eastbourne and Hastings was completed, for which 17 six-car sets were built, known as 6-PANs, complete with pantry cars staffed by Pullman Car Company stewards. In 1937, the LSWR Portsmouth direct line was electrified, followed a year later by the LBSCR Mid Sussex line to Portsmouth, and the branches to Bognor and Littlehampton. Final pre-war electrification extensions were to Gillingham, from Gravesend, and the Otford Junction-Maidstone East line, in 1939.

Below: Aldershot on July 4 1937, the first day of electrified services between Woking, Aldershot, Farnham and Alton, and also on the direct line to Portsmouth, from Guildford. Illustrated here is 4 COR unit No. 3101, a design intended chiefly for the Portsmouth route and known unofficially as either 'Pompeys' or 'Nelsons' (because of their 'one-eyed' appearance!) These were the first EMUs to have corridors throughout, and this picture was taken to highlight the SR's progress, by contrasting the brand new EMU with the ageing 'M7' at work alongside on the push-pull service to Ash.

Right, upper: A Civic reception greeted the arrival of a ceremonial opening electric train at Bognor Regis on June 30 1938, with 4 BUF set No. 3076 in attendance. These units were similar to the 4-COR type but provided buffet accommodation. At left is one of the 2 BIL units which saw widespread use on stopping trains on former LSWR and LBSCR lines.

Right, lower: An interior view of one of the buffet cars used in the 4 BUF EMU sets. The first SR vehicles to incorporate Bulleid's design ideas, these carriages were very much a 1930s style and were popular in service. One example was saved for the National Collection, but was accidentally destroyed by fire whilst on loan to a private railway.

Below: A Civic reception also awaited this inaugural train at Rochester on June 30 1939, part of the final SR electrification extensions. The Mayor of Rochester is pictured greeting the train. On this occasion the Minister of Transport had travelled down with the motorman. The rather stout gentleman next to the Town Crier was Robert Holland Martin, the SR Chairman. Apart from the lines already described, the 1939 extensions included the Guildford-Reading route and the newly-opened branch to Chessington South.

By the time of the 1938 Annual Report, the last full year of peace, there were 3,002 electric coaches and 3,618 steam coaches working on SR metals, excluding Pullman Cars. With the introduction of electric services there was great incentive for private builders to open up new residential estates near the railway, and passenger traffic consequently showed a considerable increase each year. Steam train mileage annually was about nine million miles more than the 37,500,000 miles of intensively-worked electric train mileage but the cost of the electric services was little more than the cost of steam services, which alone justified the capital expenditure required for electrification, even before the greatly increased traffic receipts which followed are taken into consideration. At the time of completion of the SR electrification in 1939, a total of 1,759 route miles had been electrified at a cost of some £20 million pounds. It was to be 20 years, well into BR days, before any capital was made available for further electrification extensions.

THAT ingenious innovator, O.V.S. Bulleid, faced with the great problem of serious overcrowding on the lines between Charing Cross or Cannon Street and Dartford, introduced two unique four-car EMU sets in 1949. Entering service on November 2, they were described, not quite correctly, as a double deck train: in practice the design was an arrangement of alternate high and low level compartments. The trains were built at the Southern Region's Lancing and Eastleigh Works, featuring all-steel construction.

Owing to restricted clearances, the windows in the upper compartments could not be opened and

THE BULLEID 'DOUBLE DECK' EMUs

pressure ventilation was used, operated by fans which drew air from the underside of the vehicles.

In service several problems immediately arose. For example, the small Bulleid wheels failed almost as soon as the train entered service, in November 1949, and although it successfully achieved a few days in service in mid-November, the original wheels had to be discarded and replaced by standard wheels of small diameter.

Because of continuing overcrowd-

ing, in spite of 1,060 seats on the train (plus 44 tip-up seats!) the ventilation proved inadequate and because there were effectively two compartments to board or alight from every door, the train had to pause for longer than was ideal at stations.

At the end of 1950, it was decided not to pursue the plan and eventually the overcrowding was resolved to a degree by the lengthening of platforms and the peak-hour provision of reinforcing the eight coach formations to ten coaches. BR did not fall into the trap of providing motorless trailers, and the extra two coaches were powered 2 EPB sets.

Above: Unit No. 4001 leads sister unit No. 4002 in an eight coach formation at Eltham, on November 2 1949, their first day in service. The train certainly presents a very distinctive appearance - and note that despite the modern outlook, a small brass organ pipe warning whistle is visible adjacent to the drivers window! The two sets were originally painted in green livery, but in the late 1960s they carried the standard BR rail blue, with overall yellow ends. From November 1970 they were renumbered 4901/2 and remained in service on the Dartford routes until withdrawal in 1971.

Left: A detail view of the Bulleid 'double deck' arrangement, at Charing Cross on November 1 1949, when the trains were displayed prior to going into service the following day. Public response to the two-level seating arrangements was poor: the lower seats were generally occupied first, whilst upper seats often remained vacant, many passengers preferring to stand. Access to the upper seats was via stairs placed centrally between the seats of the lower compartments.

SAFETY FIRST

Right: Extension of the electrified network also created problems for the Southern Railway, for whilst speed and comfort improved for the passenger, the new quiet, fast trains presented new hazards for anyone near the track. The new trains were very quiet in service and extra vigilance was required. This view, at Reading in December 1938, illustrates the point clearly. Councillor W. McIlroy, Mayor of Reading, is pictured welcoming an EMU driver, to commemorate the arrival of electric services. Of interest is the array of sternly worded signs warning passengers not to trespass on the railway, which carried much risk in view of quiet trains and the presence of live conductor rails. The post is a length of life-expired rail (nothing was wasted by the pre-Nationalisation railway companies!) whilst the upper sign is one of the traditional cast-iron variety, proclaiming that trespassers may be liable to a penalty not exceeding 40 shillings. The lower signs are of the enamel type. Note the long-armed semaphore signal arm in the background.

Left: Farmers too faced new hazards at their level crossings, and the SR took steps to ensure safety. This picture, taken in July 1939, shows a farm crossing on the London Maidstone line. A telephone had been installed, to allow the farmer to call the signalbox at Otford Junction before crossing the track with cattle or crops. To prevent unauthorised use of the crossing, farmers were given keys to the gates, which were normally kept locked. The crossings were flanked by wooden cattle grids, to stop animals straying along the railway. Once again, the warning signs are carried on a length of old rail.

Chapter 4:
CARRIAGES

LARGELY because of its long-distance services, the LSWR had the most up-to-date corridor stock of the SR constituents at the Grouping. This was the Company's so-called 'Ironclad' stock (introduced in 1921) of which construction continued until 1926, although the heavy plate-framed bogies first used on LSWR dining cars were discontinued from 1924 in favour of bogies of SECR design. From 1924, the SR's new carriage design had a closer affinity with SECR principles, not dissimilar to the 'corridor thirds' introduced in 1920.

Above: The LSWR used mobile vacuum cleaner vans to service their trains, here seen at work on a train of bogie coaches at Clapham Junction, in 1908. The two-tone salmon pink and brown livery of that time is just discernible.

Above, left: An interior view of the LSWR vacuum cleaner van, at Clapham Junction in 1908. Note that even the gleaming cylinder of the large vacuum cleaner is painted and lined to a high standard.

Above, right: Typical Wainwright coaching stock, at Charing Cross station January 1924. The open doors are those of First Class compartments where the elegant upholstery of those days is visible. Also to be seen are the antimacassars on the seats, notably in the saloon compartment. Wainwright's carriages were well designed, solidly built and quite long-lived. This was a long-distance non-corridor train. Some of the once-familiar three coach sets survived until the late 1950s.

Right: A total contrast to anything that had gone before was the continental boat train stock introduced in 1921. These massively-built coaches, provided specifically for this traffic, were initially even permitted to work on the restricted-width Hastings line, although a repeat order in 1924 was not so permitted. The occasion here is the display of the train to the Directors at Waterloo, probably the only time such stock was seen in the former LSWR terminus. Again, the antimacassars on the seat backs can clearly be seen, a reminder of a rather elegant era of rail travel. A 1924 coach of this type is preserved on the Keighley & Worth Valley Railway, 'Brake Third' No. 3554.

Left: Almost from the sublime to the ridiculous! Not luxurious by any means, but the SR was an early user of camping coaches. The first batch were conversions from 12 LCDR non-bogie coaches and they were intended to provide self-catering holidays at a suitably desirable location adjacent to a SR station, where the station staff could provide fresh water. This 1892-built coach, Camping Coach No. 7, is shown on display at Waterloo station on February 18 1935. It remained there for a week and was then exhibited at Victoria and London Bridge. The 'holiday-makers' were no doubt staff from the adjacent Headquarters offices. It is interesting to note that by the end of 1933 the SR had only 433 non-bogie coaches, the smallest number of any of the pre Grouping companies, the impoverished LNER having nearly ten times that number. The SR used them solely on summer excursions, hop pickers specials and East Kent miners trains.

Right: An interior view showing the degree of comfort provided by a former third class compartment, when converted as a bedroom with twin bunks. Fully-dressed for her role as a model, this young lady takes tea in bed for the benefit of the 'Topical' photographer. Note on the open door the once-familiar broad leather strap for opening and closing the window. The date is February 24 1936, which probably accounts for the ventilator being tightly shut. The carriage is of 1892 build. The SR's camping coaches visited a carriage maintenance depot each winter for attention, including revarnishing or 'touching up' the paintwork.

Left: On Saturday October 7 1922, more than 60,000 Boy Scouts and Cubs from all over the country assembled at the Alexandra Palace for a Review by HRH The Prince of Wales. Since office workers travelled on Saturdays at this time, the SECR must have been hard-pressed for stock, since Set 83 (seen here) was in 1922 listed as the Rotherhithe Road (Bermondsey) spare workmen's train. This is the GNR station at Wood Green, which handled more than 40 specials for this event, those from the SECR coming via Snow Hill tunnel and the Metropolitan Widened Lines. Note the Guard's 'birdcage' lookout, a distinctive SECR feature.

Below: Pullman Car *Coral* in the formation of a non-corridor Folkestone express at Charing Cross in January 1924. *Coral* was built at the Pullman Car Works at Preston Park, Brighton, in 1921 on the underframe of a former LNWR ambulance train coach. Its 8ft 6in width prevented its use through

PULLMAN CARS

the narrow tunnels of the Hastings line. *Coral* worked until 1960, when it became a Pullman camping coach; by this time holi-

daymakers expected something rather better than an 1892 non-bogie coach. SECR Third Brake No. 1367 is of interest too, for it shows the Maunsell influence on a basic Wainwright design, eliminating most of the side mouldings and the Guard's 'birdcage' roof look-out; this coach was built in 1921.

THE SR had a long association with the Pullman Car Company, mainly owing to the LBSCR, whose non-Pullman stock was for the most part undistinguished until quite late in the Company's existence. The LBSCR's Pullman connections dated back to 1875, Pullman cars having only been introduced into Britain during the preceding year by the Midland Railway, which ceased using them in 1888. The LCDR had the brief use of a single Pullman car on a Dover boat express for two years from 1882.

Whilst the LBSCR had used many single Pullman cars in its trains, in 1881 it introduced an all-Pullman train between London and Brighton, forerunner of the luxurious 'Southern Belle,' introduced in 1908. The LSWR had also experimented with the use of Pullman stock from 1882, but never had more than four cars in service at any one time; these were transferred to the LBSCR by 1912, when the LSWR decided to use its own dining cars instead.

In 1889, in connection with the Paris Exhibition, the LCDR introduced a luxury train between Victoria and Dover, the *Compagnie Internationale des Wagons Lits* providing the four saloon cars and baggage vans. The rival SER, not to be outdone, introduced similar CIWL cars in 1891, but neither service proved a financial success and, after a period in store, the

CIWL cars returned to Europe. Not discouraged, the SER introduced the 'Hastings Club Train' in 1892, using saloons built by the Gilbert Car Manufacturing Company, a rival to the Pullman Car Company in the USA. Satisfied with this service, the SER subsequently introduced the 'Folkestone Vestibule Limited' in 1897. With the working agreement between the SER and LCDR of 1899 rivalry between the companies ceased and the SECR introduced Pullman cars in 1910. After the First World War, the former SER Hastings and Folkestone trains were rebuilt as Pullmans, under the ownership of the Pullman Car Company, which since 1907 had become a British Company operating in its own right. With more than 250 Pullman cars in service by the early 1930s on all sections of the SR, there were further developments with electrically-powered Pullmans on the Brighton line from 1933, after which no new Pullmans were built until BR days.

Following the SECR Working Agreement and the transfer of the LCDR workshops to Ashford, some redundant space became available at Longhedge, Battersea and part was used from 1912 by the Pullman Car Company for carriage overhaul. All Pullman car victualling continued to be carried out there until BR days. In November 1928 the Pullman car works moved to Preston Park, Brighton, in the building pro-

Above, left: The 1891-built Gilbert Cars, although rebuilt by the Pullman Car Company in 1920 were coming to the end of their working lives, and in 1926 six new cars were built specifically for the restricted Hastings loading gauge, these being the only Pullman Cars able to work on any SR main line without restriction. Normally they were used singly and exclusively on the Hastings line, in the main expresses. On this occasion however, October 16 1929, two cars ran coupled to mark the introduction of new SR corridor stock of narrow width for use on the Hastings line. Messrs Griffiths (left) and Cox, General Manager of the Pullman Car Company and Chief Operating Superintendent of the SR discuss this innovation before departure. The other Pullman used on this occasion was *Madeline*. These cars were painted green in 1958 for use as buffet cars on Southampton liner trains, Pullman facilities having been withdrawn from the Hastings line. The car shown here is *Theodora*, preserved today by the Kent & East Sussex. Sister car *Barbara* is also preserved on the KESR.

Above, right: Edwin Cox is seen again, standing between the Mayors of Southampton and Bournemouth on the occasion of the inauguration of the daily all-year service of the 'Bournemouth Belle', January 2 1936. On the train's introduction on July 5 1931, it ran on summer service weekdays only and on Sundays in the winter service. The train used existing stock and Third Class Car No. 60, seen here, was of 1928 construction. It ended its days in the mid-1960s, latterly in the steam-hauled 'South Wales Pullman'. The 'Bournemouth Belle' ceased to run after the electrifi-

vided by the LBSCR as a paintshop. It had been made available by the run-down of Brighton Works and the transfer of carriage work to Lancing and Eastleigh. Preston Park closed in January 1964 and is now occupied by preservationists.

Left: Just a small part of the Pullman service. The 'Thanet Belle' was introduced in May 1948, and here in August of that year, 11 years old Frederick Edwards, dressed in the fashion of the original W.H. Smith newsboys, helps inaugurate a magazine and book service on Pullman car trains. The W.H.Smith company was celebrating its centenary and Master Edwards was chosen to help as he was the son and grandson of W.H. Smith employees; he was later allowed to signal the train away from Victoria. The young man is seen here selling a newspaper to passenger Miss Rosalie Edwards. Also assisting at the inauguration of this new on-train service was Miss Monica Dickens, the novelist, great grand-daughter of Charles Dickens. Indeed, her books are on sale in Master Edwards' tray!

In 1948, 'The Thanet Belle' departed for Ramsgate on weekdays from Victoria at 11.30am (3.5pm on Saturdays) calling at Whitstable, Herne Bay, Margate and Broadstairs. During the winter of 1948/9, the all-Pullman service was suspended and the train comprised ordinary stock, accompanied by perhaps two Pullman cars: all-Pullman working resumed in summer 1949. The train was renamed 'The Kentish Belle' in 1951. It still ran from Victoria to Ramsgate, but in the 1951 summer season, included through coaches to Canterbury, detached at Faversham. However, the new name was retained until the train became another casualty of electrification, for it ceased running with the inauguration of the Kent Coast scheme in 1959.

THE LSWR AMBULANCE TRAINS 1914-1918

Above: One of Urie's powerful Class H15 4-6-0s of 1913, then the largest engines on the LSWR, heads khaki green Ambulance Train No. 62, on its emergence from Eastleigh Works in May 1918. The 16-coach train weighed 440 tons (empty) and contemporary reports described the train as: "one of the finest ambulance trains in existence."

THE LSWR provided three Ambulance Trains in the 1914-18 war, most such trains being composed of 16 coaches of similar formation converted from existing stock. Typical composition was: Brake van with stores; Kitchen car; Four Ward cars; Pharmacy car; Staff car; Five Ward cars; Kitchen car; Personnel car; Ward car/brake van.

Ambulance Train No 35 was provided for the British Expeditionary Force in France, while a further train of 12 coaches was reported in use in Egypt. In the latter stages of the war, various British railway companies provided 16 trains, Nos. 51-66, for the American Expeditionary Force. The LSWR's contribution was Ambulance Train No. 62, illustrated here. Later, the LSWR also provided a demobilisation train, although in this case no internal conversion was required on the stock concerned.

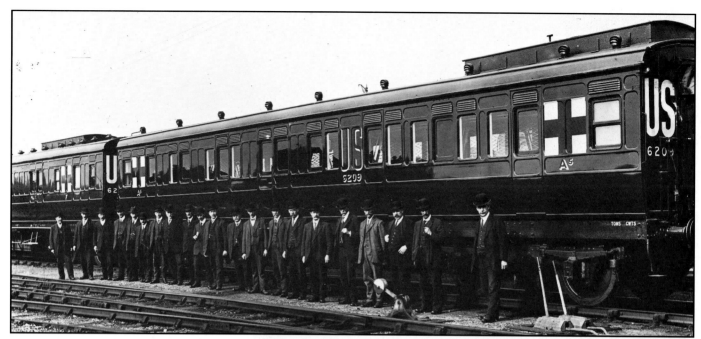

Above: A May 1918 view of LSWR staff associated with the ambulance train conversion, at Eastleigh Works, standing beside Ward Car No. 6209. Note the auxiliary water tank on the roof of this and the adjacent coach; ambulance trains carried up to 2,500 gallons of water. Car No. 6209 would be the ninth car in the train formation, the cars being numbered 6201-16, the first two digits referring to the train number. This numbering system was adopted so that in the event of vehicles being detached for repair, they could subsequently be speedily replaced at their proper place in the formation. The train featured Westinghouse continuous brakes, communication cords, international screw couplings, steam heating, electric fans and lighting, extra ventilators, tool boxes and fire extinguishers. Special footboards (visible on the adjacent coach) and boarding ladders were also provided.

Right: The interior of Ward Car No. 6214, for seriously wounded patients. Note the electric lighting and fans, and also the large number of ventilators. With the wards arranged in this way, train No. 62 could accommodate 418 persons, however, with the lower two bunks arranged as longitudinal seats (as shown on page 79) the capacity increased to 680 patients and staff. These pictures were taken at the time of the official inspection of the train by the LSWR General Manager, Sir Herbert Walker, and representatives of the American Government, for whom the train was provided.

Left: An interior view of Ward Car No. 6207, which is set out for a mixture of prone and sitting patients. Note the leather straps attached to the carriage ceiling, provided to assist patients in the upper bunks. The aspidistra was apparently provided simply for the official photographs, a strange idea since it would clearly have been an unlikely and unwelcome obstruction when the train was in use.

Below, left: The Medical Officers table in the Staff Car, laid for dinner with what is clearly the same aspidistra as shown in the ward car (left), the presence of which would certainly have hindered any conversation! It is strange to consider that in use, the ward cars might be filled with hundreds of wounded and dying men, whilst in this compartment senior medical officers were equipped to dine with linen, silver and crystal.

Below, right: Some of ambulance train No. 62's personnel, excluding the officers, posed beside Ward Car No. 6215 at Waterloo station, in May 1918. Following the official inspections at Eastleigh, the train was displayed for four days at Waterloo, one day at Kingston and two days at Bournemouth West. Members of the public paid 8d to visit the train, whilst railway staff and members of the Armed Forces paid 4d. The daily attendance at Waterloo was 2,263, 2,984, 4,050 and 2,929 over the four-day display. At Kingston, 4,207 people inspected the ambulance train, whilst at Bournemouth West the attendance figures were 4,502 and 4,740 for the two-day event. Collection boxes on the train raised more than £100 whilst 9,000 copies of a souvenir booklet were also sold; during the week of displays nearly £1,000 was raised for donation to the LSWR Servant's Orphanage, St Dunstan's Hostel for Blinded Soldiers, the St John Ambulance Association and the Fund for providing comforts for railway troops.

Right: The LBSCR built a five-coach Royal Train in 1897, primarily for the Prince of Wales, later King Edward VII. It is said that Queen Victoria did not like travelling on the LBSCR, although it was used on the occasion of her funeral, as she died at Osborne House in the Isle of Wight. Only a few special coaches on the LBSCR had clerestory roofs, but this feature was seen on the Royal Train, much-used to travel to Epsom Downs for the races. This 12-wheeled saloon was built for the Prince of Wales and Princess Alexandra, and other than Pullman cars, was the only 12-wheeled vehicle on the system. After 1923 the set was replaced by the SECR Royal Train and for two years worked a business train between Eastbourne and London each day, until new SR corridor stock was built in 1925. After this it saw only occasional special use as a First Class members race train; it was withdrawn in the early 1930s.

Above: The full rake of the LBSCR Royal Train, with an ordinary First Class carriage at the front of the formation. The 1906 Class H1 4-4-2 No. 39 (built by Kitson) was much called upon to work Royal Trains, usually between Portsmouth Harbour and Victoria. This photograph was taken on August 7 1912 and shows the Durban Royal Special near Ashtead conveying their Majesties the King and Queen.

Right: In June 1913, No. 39 was again in action and for the occasion was specially renamed *La France*. It is seen here at Portsmouth Harbour on June 24 1913, when it conveyed President Poincaré of France to London for a State Visit. The coal has been whitewashed on both occasions.

Left: HRH The Price of Wales returns home from Portsmouth Harbour, on October 11 1920. The engine was 1902-built Class B4 4-4-0 No. 46 *Prince of Wales*, an appropriate choice. This engine was designed by R.J. Billinton and was one of only two of the class to carry super-heated boilers. Despite this it was an early withdrawal, in 1936. Inevitably, electrification of former LBSCR main lines meant withdrawal of some of the Company's older engines. In view of the 'at ease' stance of the military band in the foreground, it seems that the battleship HMS *Renown* had only just berthed, and the Prince had yet to disembark In the background can be seen the Royal Yacht *Victoria and Albert,* dressed overall for the occasion.

Right: Also on October 11 1920, No. 46 *Prince of Wales* commences its journey from the Jetty with a naval party presenting arms in front of HMS *Renown.* Note that the LBSCR has not only provided a board decorated with the Prince of Wales 'feathers' but has similarly embellished the headcode discs; further decorations have also been added above the splashers. At this time, LBSCR engines were not provided with a lamp bracket above the centre of the buffer beam, hence No. 46 is not carrying the normal Royal Train headcode.

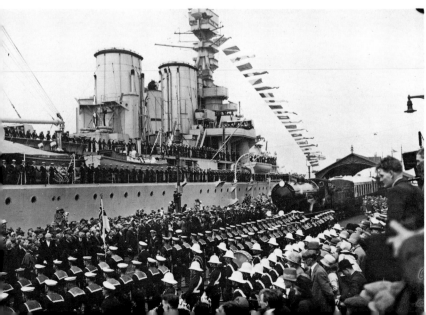

Left: Royal trains at Portsmouth Harbour did not use the public station (opened 1876) but traversed the single line South Railway Jetty, where an appropriate shelter for distinguished visitors was provided and where ships could be anchored alongside. Opened in 1878, it was originally known as the Watering Island Jetty line, being also used for troop trains. When not in use for Royal duties, it is said to have been used for empty stock. It is doubtful if the South Railway Jetty was used after 1939, as the area around Portsmouth Harbour station was severely blitzed in 1941. This view shows the return home from a six months Empire tour of their Royal Highnesses the Duke and Duchess of York, on June 27 1927. Again, HMS *Renown* had been used. By this time, Pullman cars were in use for Royal duties, for coaches built in 1902/03 for Royal use were becoming somewhat old. Unusually, Drummond 'L12' 4-4-0 No. E. 415 is in charge: a 'T9' 4-4-0 was the usual royal engine in SR days.

Above, left: On June 27 1927 (see also page 81, lower) the Royal train pulls away across the jetty line at Portsmouth, watched by numerous spectators. The Gosport ferries are doing a roaring trade. At right is one of the paddle steamers used on the service from Portsmouth to Ryde.

Above, right: Their Majesties King George VI and Queen Elizabeth arrive at Waterloo station on May 6 1939, at the start of their trip to Canada and the United States of America. The Pullman Cars used on this occasion were *Lady Dalziel*, *Cecilia*, *Marjorie* and *Montana*.

Above: Following the journey from London, HM King George VI and HM Queen Elizabeth embarked at Portsmouth for Canada and the United States of America. Here we see Queen Mary, Princess Elizabeth (waving the handkerchief, now HM Queen Elizabeth II) Princess Margaret, the Duke and Duchess of Kent, and the Duke and Duchess of Gloucester waving goodbye on the dockside, whilst in the background, immaculately cleaned Class 'T9' 4-4-0 No. 338 stands with the empty stock of the Royal train, which had arrived in the charge of 'T9' No. 718. The train had consisted of four Pullman cars and a bogie brake van, the latter visible here, at the London end of the formation. This train had not used the South Railway Jetty, but instead traversed a line into Portsmouth Dockyard to a private station adjoining the Royal Naval Barracks. In SR days, motive power for Royal train workings was usually an LSWR Drummond 'T9,' and No. 119 of this class was specially painted for this purpose, but generally eluded photographers whilst working Royal Trains. It was in fact repainted for the Royal special for the Naval Review of May 1937 (which was also the last known use of the SECR Royal train) but at the eleventh hour sister 'T9' 4-4-0 No. 716 was substituted. It is strange that on this occasion too, when a pair of beautifully-groomed 'LSWR T9' 4-4-0s were used on Royal duties, No. 119 once again did not appear.

Chapter 5:
MAUNSELL & BULLEID

RICHARD Maunsell trained on the Great Southern & Western Railway, in Ireland, as a pupil under H.A. Ivatt. After completing his training, Maunsell followed his former master to the Lancashire & Yorkshire Railway on which Ivatt became Locomotive Engineer at the age of 33. Following a brief spell in India, Maunsell returned to the GSWR in 1896, as Works Manager, at the early age of 28. His strength lay in organisation and 15 years later he succeeded R. Coey as Locomotive, Carriage & Wagon Superintendent. His tenure of office was brief as two years later he was appointed Chief Mechanical Engineer of the SECR.

He succeeded H.S. Wainwright, who was essentially more of a Carriage and Wagon Engineer, who delegated locomotive design to his assistant, Robert Surtees, a former LCDR man. No new express engines had been built since 1909 and no freight engines since 1908. Wainwright's organising ability was suspect and when the number of engines requiring heavy repair combined with ever-expanding traffic caused a large shortfall in the number of engines available to meet traffic demands in the summer of 1913, at the end of the year he was asked to resign. Maunsell took over in January 1914.

Thus, when Maunsell assumed control, affairs in the Locomotive Department of the SECR were very unsatisfactory and this was reflected in his new salary and the strengthening of his team. Within a year the country was at war and with the important ports of Dover and Folkestone to be served, the SECR was working under great pressure. Maunsell, unlike Wainwright, was a strong personality and a hard worker; he built a strong team including men of the calibre of James Clayton, from the Midland Railway, who succeeded Surtees on his retirement as Chief Locomotive Draughtsman, also G.H. Pearson

from the GWR, as Assistant CME and Ashford Works Manager. Also recruited were H. Holcroft and L Lynes, from Swindon, and C.J. Hicks, from Inchicore. Wainwright had previously occupied the additional post of Locomotive Running Superintendent but when it became obvious that he was unable to cope, this department was made independent, with A.D. Jones from the Lancashire & Yorkshire Railway in charge.

During the war, two prototype engines were designed, important designs to be much-multiplied in various forms. Heavy freight traffic on the SECR had hitherto been in the hands of Wainwright Class C 0-6-0s dating from 1900, and wartime demands had emphasised the need for more modern motive power. This came in the form of Class N 2-6-0 No. 810, marginally more powerful then Churchward's GWR Class 43xx 'Mogul' but with improved front-end design, notably in the length of valve travel. At the same time, July 1917, Class K 2-6-4T No. 790 was completed, having generally similar dimensions, apart from 6ft 0in diameter driving wheels, against the 5ft 6in wheels of No 810. Both engines proved extremely successful in service. Ashford constructed 15 more Class N 2-6-0s in 1920-3 and the Government chose the type as a suitable engine to be built at Woolwich Arsenal to maintain employment after manufacture of munitions had ceased. Boilers were provided by outside locomotive builders. Of the engines partly-built at Woolwich, the SR acquired 50 examples which were erected and completed at Ashford Works. By 1926, a further twenty 2-6-4Ts had been built, one of which was a three-cylinder engine. With the

imaginative naming policy of John Elliot, the 2-6-4Ts were named after rivers, although with the 1927 derailment of *River Cray*, the fault of the poor state of the permanent way rather than the engine, these engines were withdrawn and rebuilt as Class U 2-6-0s, losing their names in the process.

Maunsell created a little masterpiece with his 1919 rebuild of 1907 built Class E 4-4-0 with larger firegrate, high superheat and totally redesigned front end for freer steaming, this being the prototype of Class E1. These more powerful engines, no heavier than those they replaced, were desperately needed to haul heavier trains on former LCDR lines, on which the underbridges could not accept the weight of a heavier engine at that time. This became an increasingly urgent concern with the post-war transfer of all continental boat train services to Victoria. Eventually 21 Class D and 11 Class E 4-4-0s were thus rebuilt, some surviving until the end of steam traction on former SECR lines.

Maunsell's first express engine was a notable redesign of the LSWR Urie Class N15 4-6-0. the most modern express engines to be absorbed into the SR. With his former Swindon team working to improve front-end design and ensure free steaming, Maunsell was assured of success. In the event, 54 of the new 4-6-0s were built and the LSWR engines were incorporated in the class known as the 'King Arthurs'. Their rugged build and performance can be seen today in preserved example, No. 777 *Sir Lamiel*, a member of the National Collection,

Towards the end of 1923, the SR Traffic Manager announced that the heaviest expresses would load to 500 tons and run at an average speed of 55 mph whether on the South Western main line or on Continental boat expresses. The design team then started work on a four-cylinder 4-6-0, with the early Gresley 'Pacifics' and GWR 'Castles' as the existing most powerful engines. In the event, the new locomotive built at Eastleigh in 1926, No. E850 *Lord Nelson* turned out to be more powerful on a tractive effort basis than either of the GWR or LNER engines. This was rather a blow for the GWR, which had displayed a 'Castle' at the British Empire Exhibition at Wembley as 'Britain's most powerful express passenger locomotive'. At Swindon, Collett's team promptly set about designing the 'King' class 4-6-0, to regain the laurels. In fact, although *Lord Nelson* acquitted itself well on a 521-ton test train, in normal service the class was seldom called upon to haul such loads, 450 tons being more usual. When the class was multiplied to 16 examples, they were divided between Stewarts Lane and Nine Elms, from which depots they could be seen at work on two prestigious all-Pullman trains, the 'Golden Arrow' from 1929 and the 'Bournemouth Belle' from 1931. These depots in Battersea, South London, were not far apart, serving Victoria and Waterloo respectively. By this time the LCDR main line had its under-bridges strengthened to allow for heavier engines.

Above: The first SR express engines designed by Maunsell were basically an improved version of Urie's last 20 LSWR express engines, Nos. 736-55. John Elliot, the newly-appointed Public Relations Assistant to the General Manager, had the happy inspiration of naming these engines after events connected with the Court of the legendary King Arthur. Here is an early photograph of No. E453 *King Arthur*, built in 1925, leaving Waterloo on a running-in turn. Judging by the steam leaks from the engine's front end, *King Arthur* needed to return to Eastleigh Works, for attention. Nos 448-57 were built at Eastleigh, this batch having cab roofs of similar profile to the LSWR engines, rendering them incapable of working on Eastern Section lines.

It is usually said of the 'Lord Nelsons' that had there been more of them they would have been more successful. They had been designed with a very long firegrate which was flat under the firehole door and then sloping downward under the brick arch. Divided as they were between two engine sheds, not all firemen had a regular opportunity to acquire the necessary skills to become familiar with the art of firing them, and they were therefore regarded with mixed feelings by footplate

Above: Following *King Arthur*, the next 30 examples were built by the North British Locomotive Co. in Glasgow, the engines thus becoming known unofficially as 'Scotch Arthurs'. This picture purports to show the down 'Atlantic Coast Express' leaving Waterloo on July 1 1926. In fact, it is not on the Down main line and to judge from the relaxed attitude of the men on the track beside No. E776 *Sir Galagars* it is a posed picture, with a train of the new 59ft carriage stock that was about to enter service. Note that initally, Maunsell engines were not fitted with smoke deflectors; but complaints about drifting steam prompted their fitting from the early 1930s. This batch of engines was numbered E 763-792. A further 14 examples, Nos. E793-E806, were built at Eastleigh with six-wheeled tenders, for the Brighton Section. As BR No. 30776, *Sir Galagars* worked until January 1959 and was scrapped at Eastleigh.

men. After the continental boat traffic ceased on the outbreak of war in 1939 they were concentrated on the Western Section, where they proved capable of handling some very heavy wartime loads. By this time, O.V.S. Bulleid, Maunsell's successor as SR CME, had fitted them with Lemaitre multi-jet blastpipes and better front-end design, after which their improved performance left little to be desired.

Maunsell's *tour-de-force* was yet to come in the shape of the remarkable 'Schools' Class 4-4-0s, of which 40 examples were built from 1930 onwards. Designed to work through the narrow Hastings line tunnels it seems unlikely that it was envisaged that they would surpass the performance of the 'King Arthur' 4-6-0s. Not only were they the most powerful 4-4-0s in Britain but with enginemen they proved the most popular of Maunsell's locomotives. Primarily designed for former SECR lines, Nos. 924-33 went new to Fratton for the Waterloo-Portsmouth expresses and when that line was

electrified in 1937 they were transferred to Bournemouth, where they put up some of their best performances.

If Maunsell is to be remembered for his big engines, it must be the 'Schools' 4-4-0 that was his outstanding success, but his 'maids of all work' must surely not be forgotten. His two and three-cylinder 'Moguls', of which 21 were rebuilt from the 'River' Class 2-6-4Ts, eventually totalled 157. No less than 80 of these were of his first design, the Class N 2-6-0. An additional 15 Class W 2-6-4Ts were built between 1932 and 1936, using standard parts, for transfer freight trips across London, their 5ft 6in wheels enabling them to run loose-coupled freight trains as fast as possible in order to keep clear of the intensive suburban service of electric trains. Maunsell retired in 1937 at the same time as SR General Manager Sir Herbert Walker, and he was destined to be replaced as CME by a man with very different ideas. This was Bulleid, who had a shorter term

Above: A genuine picture of the down 'Atlantic Coast Express' leaving Waterloo in the charge of No. E779 *Sir Colgrevance,* on July 19 1926. This photograph was taken to show that this important train was still running following the 1926 General Strike. Normal services had resumed on May 16 but because of the continuance of the coal strike services on some lines were suspended and many cancellations were made. The General Strike had started on May 3, in support of the miners claims for increased pay and it lasted for nine days, from midnight on May 3. It was called off at 12.20pm on May 12, when a deputation of TUC leaders met Prime Minister Stanley Baldwin at No. 10 Downing Street. On the SR, although the stoppage was total at first, by the end of the strike the Company reported that 19 per cent of its passenger services were running.

of office and whose locomotives inevitably had shorter lives, with the advance of electrification and dieselisation. Most of Maunsell's engines had very long lives and survived until the early or mid-1960s. In fact, his first 'Mogul,' SECR No. 810 of 1917, had a lifespan of 47 years, in which time it ran more than one million miles.

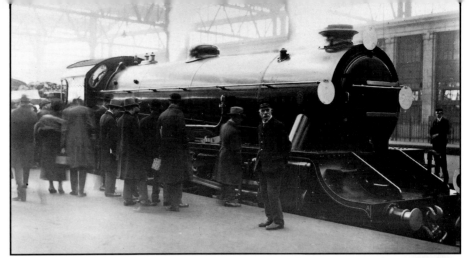

Right, upper: Railway officials inspect the new No. E774 *Sir Gaheris* at the buffer stops at Waterloo. Note the circular North British Locomotive Co worksplate on the smokebox, later hidden by smoke deflectors.

Right, lower: Trials were carried out near Byfleet, on the former LSWR main line, in October 1931 with the Strowger Hudd form of Automatic Train Control. This system was the property of a Chicago-based company, although A.E. Hudd had trained on the Lancashire & Yorkshire Railway. It relied on the engine passing over three magnets in advance of stop signals, the two latter magnets being electro-magnets activated by track circuits. With a distant signal at danger, a hooter sounded in the cab and the brakes were applied, the magnet working in conjunction with vacuum brake. The driver was able to take over control by means of a plunger, acknowledging the warning. The engine involved in the trials (on non electrified lines) was 'King Arthur' Class 4-6-0 No. 774 *Sir Gaheris*. Despite some accidents, the SR had a good safety record, second only to the GWR. The SR decided not to adopt the Strowger Hudd system, possibly foreseeing difficulties on electrified lines. It was later adopted by the LMS on its lines between Fenchurch Street and Shoeburyness, close to the Thames estuary and hence liable to disruption by fog.

Below: A crowd of officials gather around No. E850 *Lord Nelson* to see the new engine, described in the original caption as "the most powerful passenger engine in the British Isles", make a trial trip with a heavy train from Waterloo, on October 12 1926.

Left: No. 850 *Lord Nelson* is seen departing from Waterloo on October 12 1926, the same occasion as the picture shown on the opposite page (lower). The old signal box spanning the tracks, once such a familiar sight at the terminus, was demolished after the commissioning of a new power signalbox in 1937. By 1929, the class had increased to 16 engines. Withdrawn from service in August 1962 as BR No. 30850, *Lord Nelson* is preserved by the National Railway Museum as part of the National Collection.

Below: The driver of No. E860 *Lord Hawke* shakes hands with Captain Malcolm Campbell at Southampton Terminus on February 20 1931. The occasion was Captain Campbell's return from the USA after breaking the world land speed record in his car 'Bluebird', hence the special nameboard. Note the fairly elderly GWR Dean clerestory coach on the adjacent line. By then the engine had been fitted with smoke deflectors, following complaints from drivers about drifting exhaust steam and smoke obscuring their forward view.

Above: The SR held exhibitions of its latest rolling stock at principal stations from time to time. Here is one such occasion at Portsmouth & Southsea on October 21 1935, appropriately on Trafalgar Day, the obvious choice of engine for such a day was No. 850 *Lord Nelson,* which is preserved today as a member of the National Collection.

Above: Although stationary for the Portsmouth exhibition, on October 21 1935, Driver F. Knott (wearing a bow tie!) obliges the photographer by holding the regulator while Fireman J.Tilly also presents a very smart appearance in his white collar and tie. Note the electric lights, provided for the exhibition, strung along the rear edge of the cab roof, and the beautifully clean condition of the cab and its fittings.

Left: ".....and that's the driving wheel and big end..." On October 21 1933, a group of interested schoolboys are posed by the photographer with immaculately groomed No. 860 *Lord Hawke*. Note the SR practice of including the class name of the engine within the engine nameplate. *Lord Hawke* was withdrawn from service in August 1962 and scrapped within the month at Eastleigh Works.

Below: No. 855 takes water at Stewarts Lane shed, Battersea in 1936, prior to working a Continental Boat express. These were the heaviest train formations to be found on the Eastern Section, usually of 420 tons tare weight, although the 'Golden Arrow' Pullman train loaded up to 460 tons.

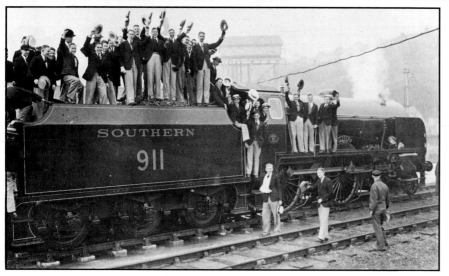

Left: Undoubtedly the most successful of Maunsell's designs was the 'Schools' Class, introduced in 1930, the most powerful 4-4-0s ever to run in Britain. Their tractive effort (25,135lb) was only slightly less than the 25,320lb rating of the larger 'King Arthur' 4-6-0s, although their adhesion weight was less. The inset cab profile permitted them to work through the narrow-bore tunnels of the Hastings line, and they were very popular wherever they went, very much an 'engineman's engine'. Where the school after which particular engines were named was situated on the SR, the new engine was sent to the nearest station for exhibition to staff and pupils. Clearly No. 911 *Dover* is appreciated by pupils of Dover College, even if the photographer has sought their attention. March 1 1933.

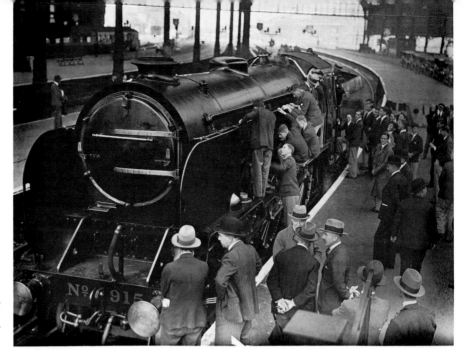

Right: On October 10 1933, staff and pupils from Brighton College inspect brand new 'Schools' 4-4-0 No. 915 *Brighton*, at Brighton station, accompanied by Sir Harry Preston, the town's mayor. This locomotive was one of the 'Schools' class engines to be fitted with a Lemaitre multi-jet exhaust and large diameter chimney by Maunsell's successor as CME, O. V. S. Bulleid. As BR No. 30915, *Brighton* was withdrawn from service in December 1962 and stored at Hove Goods Yard until the summer of 1963 when the locomotive went` to Eastleigh Works, where it was scrapped in November of that year.

Left: At Dover shed, No 934 *St Lawrence*, in standard SR green but with Bulleid lettering and numbers, is being prepared to work a special train to convey President Lebrun of France to London, for a State visit on March 21 1939. Note the French tricolor and Union Jack mounted side-by-side on each of the headcode discs. Perhaps it was thought that the French President would not be too familiar with the college at Ramsgate, so for the occasion the *Westminster* nameplates from No. 908 were substituted.

Right: Another display by the SR of one of its 'Schools' class engines to a group of interested schoolboys. This picture shows the scene at London Bridge station on July 22 1935, when No. 938 *St Olaves* was on show to pupils from the Grammar School of the same name at Tower Bridge, London. SR Director Charles Sheath presented a model of the locomotive to Mr H.E.Able, the school's headmaster. In this view, the driver is explaining the contents of the smokebox to a group of schoolboys who are illustrating the contemporary fashion (and doubtless school rules!) for turn-ups, uniform caps and strict short-back-and-sides haircuts. Inside the smokebox can be seen the jets of steam, directed up the chimney from a ring around the blastpipe cap, by the blower, which induced a draught and caused the fire to burn more brightly. The purpose was twofold: firstly to ensure that all flames, smoke and gases did not 'blow back' from the firebox into the cab, and also to create more heat from the fire during steam raising. Note also the chain provided to ensure that the heavy smokebox door did not swing open too far.

Right: The final derivative of the Maunsell 'Mogul', the Class W 2-6-4T, in this case No. 1913 at Bricklayers Arms Goods Depot, March 8 1932. The original caption describes the depot as one of the largest and most up to date in the country, and that structural alterations had been in progress over the preceding months.

Left: Maunsell's locomotives played a role of increasing importance on SR express workings in the years following the appointment of John Elliot as the country's first Public Relations Officer, in 1925. The SR had not enjoyed a very good public image and Elliot, formerly Assistant Editor of the Evening Standard, was appointed with responsibilities for advertising and publicity. He was extremely successful and his achievements included the idea of naming the Maunsell 4-6-0s of 1925 after characters asociated with the legends of King Arthur and Camelot. However, probably one of his best-known contributions was the famous poster he devised in 1925, showing a child looking up at a 'King Arthur' towering above, chatting to a friendly driver. The idea proved popular with Fleet Street's photographers, who returned to the theme again and again during the 1930s, and not simply on the SR either. This picture, taken on August 4 1933, copied Elliot's poster, the original Topical Press caption recording that the four main line companies were anticipating carrying 10 million passengers over the Bank Holiday weekend - a new record. The caption continued: "A little maiden in sun bonnet and bathing costume asks the driver of the Atlantic Coast Express at Waterloo if she is right for her seaside resort." The locomotive is 'King Arthur' No. 777 *Sir Lamiel*, now preserved as a member of the National Collection.

Unlike Richard Maunsell, Oliver Bulleid was not Irish born. Nevertheless there is a connection between the two engineers in that Bulleid started his apprenticeship in January 1901 under H.A. Ivatt, Locomotive Superintendent of the Great Northern Railway at Doncaster. His career with the GNR progressed well and by 1907 he was serving as Personal Assistant to the Works Manager at Doncaster. However, in the following year he became restless and joined the French branch of the Westinghouse Company as Chief Draughtsman and Assistant Works Manager at Freinville, near Paris.

Four years later he returned to Doncaster as Personal Assistant to Nigel Gresley, who had just succeeded Ivatt, although Bulleid was only six years younger than his chief. Bulleid served in the Army in the First World War, initially in France but latterly as Works Manager in charge of the Royal Engineers Port at Richborough, Kent with the rank of Major. On his return to Doncaster he succeeded Edward Thompson as Assistant Carriage & Wagon Superintendent.

Following the 1923 railway Grouping, Gresley was appointed Chief Mechanical Engineer of the newly-formed LNER, with Bulleid as his Assistant, being based at King's Cross. Bulleid gradually moved closer to locomotive matters and in the light of future events it is interesting to note that in 1927 he had a footplate ride on the SR's 4-6-0 No. 850 *Lord Nelson*, hauling a 455-ton continental express from Victoria to Dover, but returning with a substantially lighter load. Bulleid commented that the engine was more powerful than the work demanded and also deplored the drifting smoke and steam - smoke deflectors had not been fitted at that time.

In 1937, Sir Herbert Walker interviewed Bulleid and without delay he was appointed Chief Mechanical Engineer of the SR in place of Maunsell, who was retiring at the age of 69. Bulleid quickly set about improving the 'Lord Nelsons', fitting Lemaitre multiple-jet blastpipes and modifying the front-end design, including the provision of 10in piston valves. These changes greatly improved the 'Nelson's' performance. Lemaitre blastpipes were also fitted to some of the 'Schools' 4-4-0s, but in view of the already outstanding performance of these engines, it is questionable whether this brought about any improvement and only half the class were so-treated.

Bulleid was determined to accelerate steam schedules on a railway which had concentrated on electrification for so long, to the detriment

of its steam-hauled services. He also decided to brighten the SR's image by substituting the brighter malachite green in place of sage green on passenger engines and carriages. He was also faced with the situation that only 28 new steam locomotives had entered traffic between 1933 and 1937, although 20 engines of Maunsell's general purpose Class Q 0-6-0s entered traffic in 1938-9.

Bulleid was determined to build a more powerful express locomotive of 4-6-2 design and an initial attempt at an air-smoothed version was on the drawing board early in 1938. The main reason behind this proposal was the increasing demands of the Dover boat trains, but he had to take into account the 21 tons maximum axle loading imposed by the SR Civil Engineer, George Ellson, who had been appointed shortly before the Sevenoaks derailment of 1927 and whose actions had been coloured by it ever since. The 4-6-2s were authorised as early as March 1938 and a remarkably free-steaming boiler was designed with a large grate area and the (at that time) record boiler pressure of 280psi. The coupled wheel diameter of 6ft 2in was less than that usually featured on express passenger locomotives; it coincided with the driving wheel diameter of the LNER Gresley Class V2 2-6-2s whose ability to run at speed had not been impaired. Because of the outbreak of war there were inevitably delays before the first locomotive was completed, but because much of the required material was conveniently to hand, its construction went ahead. The class was to be known as the 'Merchant Navy' Class and Bulleid thrust aside conventional numbers in favour of a variation of the French system. The first two digits indicated the number of leading and trailing axles, a single letter indicated the number of coupled wheels, whilst the final digit indicated the engine's number within the class. Thus, the pioneer 'Merchant Navy' became No. 21C1. The engine was named *Channel Packet* in honour of the SR's own merchant seamen, many of whom attended the naming ceremony. Inevitably, Ellson had judged the design too heavy and weight had to be reduced by three tons.

For these engines, Bulleid evolved a totally new chain-driven valve gear encased in an oil bath. This was as a result of having seen at first hand the incidence of overheated bearings on the LNER. He was therefore reluctant to use Gresley's type of derived motion for the inside cylinders, nor could he easily fit Walschaerts motion in the restricted space on an engine where the connecting rod drove on to the second coupled axle, bearing in mind the short wheelbase.

There were inevitably some teething troubles with the new locomotive, but as the crews and fitters became more familiar with them, these were overcome. Only the first four examples carried malachite green livery, Nos. 21C5-19 entering service in the wartime black livery current on all SR engines. In the event, this was rather more in keeping with some the early work of the class, on freight trains, notably on heavy night trains between Nine Elms and Exeter. Their use on goods trains was partly in order that the SR could keep faith with its claim that the class was intended for mixed traffic use, but Bulleid welcomed this as it provided an opportunity to resolve early problems away from the public scrutiny of express passenger service.

From 1943 a cowl was fitted ahead of the chimney, thus improving the drifting of steam, the design resulting from tests with a scale model in

a wind-tunnel at Southampton University, using vaporised paraffin to simulate steam and smoke. The first ten engines were in service by July 1942 and much of their work was carried out on freight duties between London or Southampton and Salisbury, while they were also put to work on the very heavy passenger trains then required on the West of England line out of Waterloo.

Bulleid had decided that much of the SR locomotive stock was obsolete, electrification having taken priority over the construction of new steam locomotives, hence his decision to start design work on a class of lightweight 4-6-2s with the ability

to work over much of the system.

Before that however, the exigencies of wartime traffic had shown the desperate need for more powerful 0-6-0s, with an equally wide route availability. All non-essential items were ruthlessly omitted and the wartime keynote was austerity; besides the engine had to receive Ellson's approval. The result was the most powerful 0-6-0 seen in Britain but the least pleasing aesthetically. Nevertheless, the 40 'Q1s' made a valuable contribution to the war effort and indeed subsequently. The Southern Region must have been rather pleased with the design as it chose to donate the prototype

engine, SR No. C1, by then BR No. 33001, to the National Collection. At the time of going to press, it is based on the Bluebell Railway, where it is maintained in working order at Sheffield Park, although in Spring 1988 the locomotive was undergoing overhaul.

The first lightweight 4-6-2, No. 21C101 *Exeter* appeared in 1945, the class then being announced as the 'West Country' class, and 66 of the engines eventually built by 1951 were so named, the remainder forming the 'Battle of Britain' class, appropriate since most of the battle had been fought over Kent. These engines all had a widespread route

Below: No. 21C1 *Channel Packet* is named at Eastleigh by Lt. Col. Moore-Brabazon (later Lord Brabazon), the Minister of Transport, in the presence of many railway officials; Bulleid is standing on the platform in a double-breasted overcoat, looking at the nameplate. Sir Ralph Wedgwood was present from the LNER and whilst Sir Nigel Gresley, Bulleid's former chief, had been invited he was ill and sadly died three weeks later. Note the sailors present amongst the party, also the small ships wheel embellishing the platform.

Above: Wearing a footplateman's cap for the benefit of the photographer, Lt. Col. Moore-Brabazon poses in the fireman's cab window of No. 21C1. Standing behind the Minister of Transport, smiling rather proudly it seems, is Oliver Bulleid. *Channel Packet* had been completed in February as the SR's first 'Pacific' locomotive, although it had been necessary to classify the 'Merchant Navy', which was quite clearly an express passenger locomotive, as a mixed traffic design in order to secure government approval to proceed with construction in time of war.

Above: Having successfully hauled 20-coach test trains, *Channel Packet* leads its three-coach train of VIPs to Alresford, following the formal naming at Eastleigh, in March 1941. The leading coach is the former LBSCR Officers Saloon, which survived well into BR days and is now preserved on the Bluebell Railway.

availability. No 4-6-0, for example was allowed to cross Meldon Viaduct, beyond Okehampton, to reach Plymouth, a 4-4-0 or 2-6-0 taking expresses west from Exeter before construction of the 'West Country' class. These engines put up some remarkable performances on express trains, but with so many of them in traffic (110 in all) they were also

seen on relatively light duties. It was often difficult to find appropriate express work for them all.

Bulleid's last steam design was less successful, and although design started earlier, the first material was ordered in 1946 for five 'Leader' class tank engines of a revolutionary design. Only one example was ever completed, although two others

were partly built before the project was scrapped. The original engine, No. 36001, took part in test runs in

Left, upper: An interesting elevated view of No. 21C1 at Alresford, during the trial run of March 11 1941. Strange to think that all these years later, Bulleid 'Pacifics' are still a common sight on this particular piece of railway! This view gives a revealing perspective on the upper smokebox plating as originally applied to the 'Merchant Navy' class: note the horizontal slot located above the smokebox door (see also rear cover illustration) through which air was ducted to the transverse slot immediately in front of the chimney cavity. The idea was that at speed this movement of air would lift the exhaust smoke and steam clear of the boiler casing: as shown on the opposite page, this did not work, and the drivers forward view was obstructed. Note also the circular cover which could be slid into position over the chimney, presumably to keep the smokebox dry whilst the locomotive was out of service.

Left, lower: An impressive low viewpoint of the pioneer Bulleid 'Pacific' at Alresford, clearly showing the distinctive Bulleid-Firth-Brown 'Boxpok' wheels and the self-adjusting brakes, which acted on both sides of the driving wheels. The air-smoothed casing, was designed not so much for its streamlined qualities, as to facilitate cleaning by mechanical equipment, similar to that used for carriages and indeed locomotives today.

1949 and 1950, the project then being abandoned, after Bulleid's departure. Being unsympathetic to many of the results of railway Nationalisation, Bulleid retired from BR in September 1949, after which he became Consulting Engineer of CIE, in Ireland, until 1958, when a further spate of government interference caused him finally to retire. Bulleid was an individualist but he certainly transformed the SR motive power scene. In BR days all the 'Merchant Navy' class and 60 of the 'West Country' and 'Battle of Britain' classes were rebuilt as more orthodox 4-6-2s. The rebuilt 'Merchant Navy' class engines, and the so-called 'light' Pacifics in both original and rebuilt forms are popular in preservation, thanks jointly to the existence of Barry scrapyard and the dedication of enthusiast groups. It would probably be fair to say that there are as many admirers of Bulleid 'Pacifics' as those of Gresley 'Pacifics'.

Steam traction ended on the Southern Region in 1967 with electrification of the Bournemouth line, and even in their last rather run-down years, Bulleid's engines put up some remarkable high speed performances.

WITH one exception, the photographs of 'Merchant Navy Pacifics' which follow are of naming ceremonies. About one-third of the class of 30 engines have been preserved, No. 35028 *Clan Line* was fortunate enough to escape sale for scrap and is a regular main line approved running locomotive. No. 35029 *Ellerman Lines* is sectionalised at the National Railway Museum, in York, whilst other examples have been rescued from Barry scrapyard. On the Mid Hants Railway, where examples of both original and rebuilt 'light Pacifics' can be seen, No. 35018 *British India Line* was undergoing restoration as this book went to press. No. 35027 *Port Line* was steamed for the first time, after restoration from scrapyard condition, in Spring 1988. Fourteen members of the class, which worked until the last days of steam on the Southern region, in 1967, attained more than a million miles in service, a creditable achievement.

Right: The naming ceremony of No, 21C2 *Union Castle* at Waterloo in 1941, when even the railway officers carried gas masks and steel helmets, while the assembled service and ARP personnel are no doubt from the staff of the SR. Unlike the other three main line railways, the SR had its own Home Guard Battalion staffed entirely by its own personnel. No. 21C2 is fitted with the inverted horseshoe 'Southern' roundel on the smokebox door, accompanied by a large cast numberplate. As BR No. 35002, *Union Castle* was rebuilt in May 1958 and worked until February 1964, after which the locomotive was stored at Nine Elms. It was scrapped by the Slag Reduction Company, Rotherham, in December 1964.

Above: The formal naming of No. 21C2 *Union Castle* at Waterloo. The gentleman looking in the photographer's direction is SR General Manager Eustace J. Missenden, who at Nationalisation was appointed Chairman of the Railway Executive.

Right: A group of permanent way men stand clear as No. 21C3 *Royal Mail* passes, with four carriages and a Class M7 0-4-4T on the rear, as it enters Waterloo for its naming ceremony in 1941. Note that the circular cast roundel had been fitted to the smokebox door and that the front number is now painted above the buffer beam.

Left: On the right, the station's business goes on as usual on October 24 1941 at Waterloo, whilst alongside No. 21C3, the official party stands quietly prior to the unveiling of the *Royal Mail* nameplates. This view shows clearly the modified smoke-clearing arrangements incorporated by Bulleid, following experience with No. 21C1 *Channel Packet*. The horizontal air duct above the smokebox door has been much enlarged, in an attempt to increase the airflow and lift exhaust clear of the air-smoothed plating. Interestingly, on the opposite page, No. 21C3 is seen travelling into Waterloo in the opposite direction to that shown here. A photographer has squeezed into a very dangerous position between the locomotive and the platform whilst on the extreme left, one of his colleagues from the press corps is seen taking notes of the speeches.

Above: No. 21C3 stands outside the station at Waterloo, the subject of admiring glances from the permanent way men alongside. Compared to the existing front line motive power (the 'Lord Nelson', 'King Arthur' and 'Schools' classes) Bulleid's new creation must have indeed been a strange and impressive sight. Once initial teething troubles were resolved, the 'Merchant Navy' 4-6-2s did marvellous work with heavy wartime trains, albeit at the cost of heavy fuel consumption.

Left: After the naming ceremony, Lord Essendon, Chairman of the Royal Mail company, stands besides the locomotive wearing brand new, rather ill-fitting overalls and is clearly looking forward to a footplate ride. Standing next to him is Robert Holland-Martin, the SR Chairman. Note the small sliding access panel in the boiler casing, and the row of holes in front of the drivers window, giving access to the Belpaire firebox washout plugs.

Above: No. 21C5 *Canadian Pacific* stands at Victoria station on March 28 1942, on the occasion of its formal naming by F.W. Mottley, Acting European Manager, Canadian Pacific Railway Company. The smokebox roundel reveals that the locomotive was completed at Eastleigh in 1941 and it was not unusual for locomotives to run for some weeks with its nameplates covered, until a suitable ceremony could be arranged. No. 21C5 is in very clean condition, as might be expected, and the electric headlights are all lit. This view also shows the modified air ducting around the chimney, designed to lift smoke clear of the locomotive. This engine is one of the survivors: *Canadian Pacific* was rebuilt in May 1959, withdrawn as BR No. 35005 in October 1965 and subsequently delivered to Woodham's of Barry, for scrap. However, it was purchased for preservation and transferred to Steamtown, Carnforth in 1973.

Above, left: The left-side nameplate of No.21C4 *Cunard White Star*, photographed on January 1 1942 at the naming ceremony at Charing Cross, performed by Sir Percy Bates, Chairman of Cunard White Star Ltd. The original Topical Press caption describes No. 21C4 as: "a mixed traffic locomotive of the 'Merchant Navy' class," thereby perpetuating the belief that the new 'Pacifics' were not express passenger locomotives, as which they had been originally designed in 1938. It is also of interest to recall that the nameplates were cast in both left and right-handed versions, to ensure that the company house flags always 'fluttered' in the correct direction when the engines were at work.

Above, right: Construction of the 'Merchant Navy' class at Eastleigh continued until 1949, and Nos. 35021-35030 emerged into traffic under BR auspices, in Brunswick green livery, lined in black and orange. No. 35025 *Brocklebank Line* was named at Waterloo on September 20 1949, and pictured here is Brocklebank Line chairman Col. Denis H. Bates (right) unveiling the nameplate. On the left is R.P. Biddle, Docks and Marine Manager, Southampton. No. 35025 was rebuilt in December 1956 and withdrawn in September 1964 after which it was despatched to Woodham's scrapyard, Barry. It has since been rescued and at the time of going to press awaited restoration at the Great Central Railway, where it is regarded as a long term project. The Bulleid 'Pacifics' have been extremely attractive to preservationists, and following the purchase of the last surviving locomotives from Woodham's yard, at Barry Island, South Wales, 31 examples were preserved, with an increasing number to be found in working order, as the years pass.

Above: 'Merchant Navy' No. 21C4 *Cunard White Star* was appropriately chosen to haul the first post-war boat express out of Waterloo for Southampton Docks on October 18 1946 for the first passenger voyage of the RMS *Queen Elizabeth*, all her previous voyages having been made as a troopship. Note that by this time, for this prestigious occasion No. 21C4 had lost its wartime black for the splendour of malachite green livery. The improved cowl in front of the chimney, by then fitted to all members of the class, can also be seen.

Left: Towards the end of the war, Bulleid was working on a lightweight version of the 'Pacific' design, intended for use on the SR's restricted secondary routes over which the 'Merchant Navy' class could not operate. The weight was reduced by around ten tons to 86 tons, with a correspondingly lighter tender, but the finished product looked little different to their bigger shedmates. The first three 'light Pacifics' emerged from Brighton Works in Summer 1945. The class was given names of places in Cornwall, Devon, Dorset, Somerset and Wiltshire, the first being No. 21C101 Exeter. Here we see 'West Country' Class 4-6-2 No. 21C119, built in December 1945 and later named *Bideford*, entering London Bridge with a down Ramsgate express on February 27 1946. The previous 18 engines of the class were allocated to the Western Section and this was the first of its type to work on the Eastern Section. This engine only saw a short spell of service on Kent Coast lines, after which it was soon replaced by a later-built engine. No. 21C119 then went to Exmouth Junction, more appropriate to its name.

Above: An official view of No. 21C151 *Winston Churchill*. This locomotive, one of a batch of locomotives (Nos. 21C149-21C170) built at Brighton Works during 1946/47, was completed during 1946. This locomotive was used to haul Winston Churchill's funeral train in 1965 and is now preserved at the National Railway Museum, York, as part of the National Collection. In BR days, the 'Battle of Britain' 4-6-2s were numbered 34049-90 and 34109/10, this locomotive becoming No. 34051. The 44 'Battle of Britain' locomotives combined with the 66 'West Country' examples to create an overall class of 110 engines.

Right, upper: No. 21C157 *Biggin Hill* is named at Waterloo on February 24 1948 by Sir Archibald Sinclair, who was Secretary of State for Air from 1940 until 1945. Standing on the left is John Elliot, SR Chief Regional Officer, whilst on the right is Squadron Leader G.D. Sise DSO DFC, Station Commander at RAF Biggin Hill. John Elliot followed an early career in journalism with a distinguished railway career, and succeeded Sir Eustace Missenden as Chairman of the Railway Executive and ultimately received a knighthood. As BR No. 34057, this locomotive worked until May 1967 and was subsequently scrapped by Cashmore's, of Newport, in December of the same year.

Right, lower: A proud moment for Sir Archibald Sinclair. After naming No. 21C159 *Sir Archibald Sinclair*, also on February 24 1948, the Secretary of State for Air donned a footplateman's greasetop cap and posed in the fireman's cab window for the benefit of the photographers. Sir Archibald certainly cuts an impressive figure in his immaculate wing collar and bow tie - but the engine crew appear rather reluctant to enter into the spirit of the occasion! At this time, a final decision on BR engine renumbering had yet to be made and temporarily SR engines as repainted carried the prefix 'S'. This locomotive is preserved today on the Bluebell Railway and in Spring 1988 was still undergoing restoration to working order.

Sir Eustace Missenden was General Manager of the SR from 1939 to 1947, when he became the first Chairman of the Railway Executive. He was thus in charge when the SR was in the front line during the Second World War. Consequently, he had the privilege of unveiling the nameplate of No. 34090 *Sir Eustace Missenden* at Waterloo on February 15 1949, as a representative of all grades of Southern Railway men who had achieved so much in the conflict. The engine was on display at an Ashford Works Open Day on August 31 1949, as shown on this page where it was clearly much-admired. An excursion from London to Ashford for the occasion cost 7/6d per ticket. Above: A lengthy queue forms for a short footplate ride, whilst on the right, engines in the Works yard include an SECR Class H 0-4-4T and two LBSCR 0-6-2Ts. Left: A rear three-quarter view of No. 34090 and a group of interested visitors, mainly young boys. No. 34090 worked until the last hours of steam on Southern metals: it was withdrawn in July 1967 and was scrapped by Cashmore of Newport in March 1968.

Chapter 6:

PASSENGER TRAINS

THE GWR and SECR joint service between Birkenhead and the Kent Coast was introduced as a permanent part of the timetable in July 1903, following preliminary trials.

Nevertheless, it was a victim of severe service cuts on the SECR in 1916 and was not resumed until July 10 1922. Each company provided coaches and for the SECR, the 15 composite First/Third Class brake coaches built at Ashford in 1907 for its through trains to the GWR LNWR and MR were its first gangway corridor coaches. No further corridor coaches were built by the SECR until 1920, when six 'Corridor Thirds' were completed, some of which appeared on the Birkenhead service. The SECR worked the train to and from Reading over its own line through Guildford, quite steeply graded in parts, notably on that part of the lines west of Redhill, where the train had to reverse. These pictures, actually taken in October 1922, purport to show the opening of the service, which took place in July.

FROM BIRKENHEAD TO THE KENT COAST

Above: As noted elsewhere, the line from London Bridge to Redhill was jointly worked by the LBSCR and SECR. The Brighton line ran straight through, but the junction lines were those of the SECR. Thus, the route from Reading and Guildford came in on the Up side, where the train reversed to take the Tonbridge line on the Down side, inevitably involving conflicting movements across the through lines. The LBSCR built the deviating Quarry Line in 1900 avoiding the Coulsdon-Redhill line because of the delays that tended to occur by the junction working at Redhill. This part of the line was owned by the SECR under the 1842 agreement between both companies. Rebuilt Stirling 4-4-0s, No. 88 and 74, round the curve into Redhill, in October 1922. These 1890s engines each had a lifespan of about 40 years.

Facing page, lower: The train at rest in Redhill station, looking north. The carriage destination board reads 'Birkenhead, Chester, Birmingham, Oxford, Canterbury, Ramsgate and Margate'. At this time, this portion ran over the former SER line into the terminus at Margate Sands, involving a further reversal at Ramsgate Town. After the SR's rationalisation of the former competing LCDR and SER lines in Thanet in July 1926, this train called at the new Ramsgate through station, both LCDR and SER termini having been closed, and fol-lowed a spur connection to the LCDR's line through Broadstairs to that company's rebuilt Margate West station. The SER's route to Margate Sands was closed, apart from a goods yard at Margate. Two coaches of this train were detached at Redhill to run to Hastings, two coaches ran through to Margate Sands and the main part of the train having called at Folkestone and Dover, terminated at Deal. In the immediate foreground, two typical SECR bogie coaches. Note the 'birdcage' Guards look-out on the rearmost coach.

Above: Ready to leave Redhill, the Birkenhead-Kent coast train has been reversed and is in the charge of Wainwright Class D 4-4-0 No. 549 of 1906. The two leading coaches of SECR design (the second of which is one of the corridor composite brakes) were through coaches from Bournemouth West to Margate, attached to the rear of the train at Guildford. Reboilered Stirling Class B1 4-4-0 No. 440 stands in the down platform on a stopping train. The impressive array of semaphore signals is of much interest, for until SR days, distant signals on the SECR (and also the LBSCR and LSWR) displayed a white light when in the 'off' position. This was considered unsatisfactory in the early 1900s, when these companies decided to use the Coligny-Welch patent fishtail reflector to indicate that the signal was a distant, irrespective of whether the arm was 'on' or 'off.' These reflectors can be seen to the right of the posts carrying the distant signals of the right hand gantry.

RACE SPECIALS

REMARKABLY, at its formation in 1923, the SR found that it served no fewer than 23 racecourses, not all of which are still in existence today.

No doubt the most famous of these was Epsom, served by all three companies, the LBSCR and LSWR at the joint Epsom station (after the LBSCR's Epsom Town had closed in 1929), the LBSCR at Epsom Downs and the SECR at Tattenham Corner.

Left: Drummond Class L11 4-4-0 No. 155 leaving Waterloo on an 104 Race Special in June 1923. This was one of 40 engines of this class built between 1903 and 1907 and one of eight to have at that time a six-wheeled tender, more familiar on the similar but smaller Class K10. The stock consists of non corridor coaches. Note the solitary milk churn at right; milk traffic was later transferred to Vauxhall. The repainted vehicle in the assorted van train at right proclaims itself to be a Meat Van.

In the week after the opening of the Nine Elms terminus, the LSWR advised that it would run eight special trains to Kingston on Derby Day. When the station opened for business that day, the officials, barely used to running a railway, let alone organising excursions, were dismayed to find a crowd of about 5,000 hopeful people assembled. Several trains left the station, which must have taxed existing rolling stock availability to the utmost. By noon the crowds were increasing and there were no more trains, so the police had to be summoned to control the situation.

Undaunted in spite of this experience, a few weeks later special trains to Woking (for Ascot Races) were advertised.

The other principal racecourses served were: **LSWR**: Exeter, Fontwell Park, Hurst Park, Kempton Park, Salisbury, and Sandown Park; **LBSCR**: Brighton, Gatwick, Goodwood, Lewes, Lingfield and Plumpton. **SECR**: Folkestone and Wye. **IOW**: Ashey.

Both the LBSCR and the SECR ran all-Pullman trains on Derby Day and the service to Tattenham Corner continued to run into the 1950s.

The SR maintained in pre-war days sets of First Class coaches which only saw service a few days a year as Members Race Trains.

Gatwick Racecourse was adjacent to the field that served as Gatwick Aerodrome in 1930 and was served by a four-platform station, built by the LBSCR in 1891 and only opened on race days. With the expansion of Gatwick Airport the racecourse closed down.

Above: The SECR line from Purley to Tadworth opened in 1900 and was extended to Tattenham Corner for Epsom Downs race traffic in 1901, in competition with the LBSCR route to Epsom Downs. Racing at Epsom ceased during the First World War, when the station was used for military traffic and later for the storage of Railway Operating Division 2-8-0s of GCR design following use in France. They were brought back via the train ferry to Richborough, awaiting sale. This is Derby Day at Tattenham Corner in May 1922 with Class N 2-6-0s Nos. 812 and 817 in charge of Pullman race specials from Charing Cross. At right, the sidings are full of horse boxes, a once valuable traffic. Right into the 1960s a special horse box train brought mounted police to the Derby course on the most important race days, usually to Epsom Downs. Public services, apart from race days, did not commence to Tattenham Corner until after electrification in 1928.

Right: A wet day outside the LBSCR's Epsom Downs station as punters hurry to join their trains.

Left: In dull conditions prior to electrification in June 1928, passengers join their train after a damp day's racing, at Epsom Downs in 1928. The grassed platform on the right was a spare platform used only on race days, and the non-corridor train shown here is comprised of LBSCR stock. This station also had an abundance of carriage sidings, and after electrification an LBSCR locomotive fitted with Westinghouse brakes was rostered here on race days, to shunt electric stock into non-electrified sidings. Note that former LBSCR catering had been provided by Bertram & Co. General Manager Sir Herbert Walker was set firmly against the railway providing catering facilities, preferring instead to take a percentage from outside contractors. When the contracts of Bertram & Co and Spiers & Pond expired, the SR catering contract (for non-Pullman refreshments) went to Frederick Hotels Ltd.

THE GOLDEN ARROW

Above: The SS *Canterbury* ready to sail to Dover, at Calais, on May 17 1929, soon after its entry into service on the inauguration of the 'Golden Arrow' service.

IN 1929 the SR introduced a new cross-Channel steamer, the SS *Canterbury* a 2,912-tons vessel built at William Denny's Dumbarton yard. This luxury steamer was reserved exclusively for passengers on the 11.00 Victoria-Dover and 12.00 Paris Nord-Calais, the London-Paris time in each direction being 6hrs 35mins. The French

Below, left: Platform 8, the usual departure platform at Victoria for the 'Golden Arrow' was given some special treatment to publicise the train, including this eye-catching arch over the ticket barrier.

Below, right: On the platform, the Conductor gives instructions to the immaculately attired Stewards at Victoria, before the inaugural post-war run of April 13 1946. Note that at this time the Pullman cars carried the legend 'Golden Arrow' at each end, a feature that had previously been lacking. The prestige nature of the service is clearly evident from the polished coachwork to the conductors brilliantly shined shoes!

train 'Le Fléche d'Or' had been provided with British-built luxury coaches, initially in Pullman colours, from September 1926. On the English side an all-Pullman train was also provided in September 1926, although at that time it did not have the distinction of a name. It left Victoria daily at 10.45am followed by an ordinary train, thereby enabling the Pullman passengers to have first choice of seats on the steamer! The ordinary train ceased three years later when the SS *Canterbury's* accommodation was designated exclusively for 'Golden Arrow'/'Fléche d'Or' passengers.

Lord Davison Dalziel owned the Pullman Car Company in Great Britain and was Chairman of the European CIWL, hence to coincide with SS *Canterbury's* introduction the British train was named the 'Golden Arrow', a First Class only Pullman train inaugurated on May 15 1929. Hand baggage was quickly examined between train and ship at Dover and on the train in France, while passengers handed the keys of heavy luggage to a railway represen-

tative for Customs examination. Such luggage was subsequently delivered by road motor in either capital the same evening.

Within months of the train's introduction, the world depression took place and from 1931 the number of Pullmans was reduced and ordinary SR First and Second Class coaches were substituted - at this time SR trains provided First and Third Class accommodation, and only the boat trains provided for Second Class passengers. Haulage of the 'Golden Arrow' was almost

Right: The trial run recorded at speed en route in the charge of No 21C1 *Channel Packet*. This view clearly shows the 'Golden Arrow' and 'Fléche D'Or' insignia and arrows applied to the Pullman cars.

Left: Passengers boarding the SS *Canterbury* at Dover on April 15 1946, on its return to normal 'Golden Arrow' service, although this was to be short-lived with its impending replacement by the SS *Invicta*. The *Canterbury* was 342ft in length and its accommodation was designed with its 'Golden Arrow' clientele firmly in mind: the vessel provided private cabins and featured a number of screened-off alcoves, giving an atmosphere of semi-privacy for groups of passengers travelling together. Total capacity was 1,400 passengers.

Right: Stewards wait for the 'Golden Arrow' passengers in Platform 8 at Victoria station, October 13 1947, beside Pullman Car *Onyx*, built in 1928. By this time, according to the original Topical Press Agency caption, the train was running half-empty, although it tended to be less busy in the winter months. At this time, the usual 'Golden Arrow' formation comprised ten Pullman cars and a pair of vans.

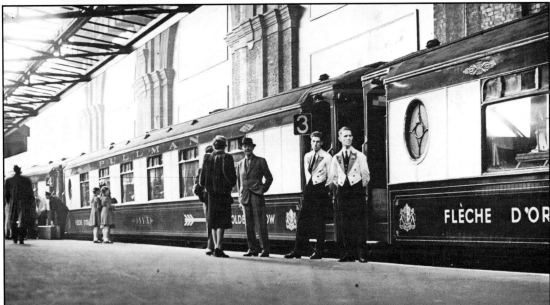

Left: On October 11 1946, Conductor Goodman of the 'Golden Arrow' formally presented a gold brooch and a sprig of flowers to the 100,000th passenger to travel on the train since its restoration six months earlier.

invariably entrusted to a 'Lord Nelson' Class 4-6-0. Inevitably, the service was withdrawn following the outbreak of war in September 1939, and during the war the Pullman cars were stored.

At the end of the war in Europe, the Pullman Car Company devoted all its efforts towards the resumption of the 'Golden Arrow' service. Hence, the first post-war Pullman Cars to run in Britain were on the restored 'Golden Arrow,' which recommenced running on April 15 1946 when its French CIWL counterpart also resumed operation on the 'Fleche d'Or'. There was a press and VIP run on April 12 1946 when Bulleid's first 'Merchant Navy' Class 4-6-2 No. 21C1 *Channel Packet* was in charge.

For the Channel crossing, the SS *Canterbury* was again available, after distinguished wartime service, including the evacuation of Dunkirk and the D-Day landings in Normandy. Departure from Victoria was at 10.00am with a formation of ten Pullman Cars and two vans. The post-war service was slower than the original timing. Six months later on October 15 1946 the famous SS *Canterbury* was replaced by the SS *Invicta*, at 4,178 tons the largest cross Channel steamer of its day. Launched by Denny's at the end of 1939 this ship, like its predecessor had a distinguished wartime career including the Dieppe raid and the Normandy landings. Originally designed to burn Kent coal, she was converted to oil-burning in 1946 prior to entry into SR service. SS *Canterbury* was then transferred to the Folkestone-Boulogne route.

In pre-war days the 'Lord Nelson' Class 4-6-0s had been divided between Nine Elms and Stewarts Lane sheds, operating on former LSWR and SECR lines respectively. With the ending of boat train traffic in wartime, they were all transferred to former LSWR lines on which the heaviest trains were running.

The post-war 'Golden Arrow' services were largely in the hands of Bulleid 'Pacifics', mainly of the 'West Country' or 'Battle of Britain' classes, with the occasional appearance of a 'Merchant Navy', the latter engines usually being assigned to the heavier 'Night Ferry' duties. However, between late 1951 and the end of the 1957-8 winter train service, two BR 'Britannia' 4-6-2s were allocated to Stewarts Lane and unless unavailable, one of these would be diagrammed for the duty.

Seven new First Class Pullman Cars and three refurbished Second Class Pullmans were introduced to the 'Golden Arrow' in 1951. Latter-day Pullmans were built by various Birmingham carriage builders, but the internal fitting-out, veneered wood panelling and furnishing was entirely the work of the Pullman Car Company's Preston Park Works at Brighton. In the winter of 1952-3 the Victoria departure was changed to 2.00pm and the outward service ran via Folkestone and Boulogne. The Pullmans were then worked empty to Dover to meet the ship arriving from Calais, this being a complete reversal of the immediate pre-war procedure. In June 1961 the 'Golden Arrow' went over to electric locomotive haulage until the end of September 1972 when it was finally withdrawn. Four of the 1951 cars are now in the ownership of VSOE Ltd and two are in the regular formation of the 'Venice Simplon Orient Express'.

THE SS 'AUTOCARRIER'

Right: The SS *Autocarrier* is of interest in being the first SR cross-Channel ship built after the *Canterbury*, entering service in 1931. She was originally intended to be a cargo ship, but as Townsend Ferries had recently introduced a car ferry on the cross channel service, the SR decided to meet the competition head on with a vessel designed specifically for the carriage of 35 cars and their passengers. The SS *Autocarrier*, of 822 tons weight, was built by D & W Henderson, Glasgow in 1931. Her maiden voyage was on March 30 1931, when the only car shipped to France was Earl Howe's aluminium and blue 3.5 litre Mercedes racing car, seen here ready to be loaded aboard the ship. The special train from London was hauled to Dover by 'Lord Nelson' class 4-6-0 No. 857 *Lord Howe*, whose crew are watching the proceedings with interest. In service, the vessel sailed daily between Calais and Dover, the fare for passengers accompanying cars being ten shillings, the rate for cars varying (according to wheelbase) from £1. 76. 6. to £5.

TRAIN Ferries on the English Channel began towards the end of the First World War, from the temporary military port at Richborough, Kent, to Calais, a 31-miles crossing. Three vessels were built for the service, the military unimaginatively calling them TF1. TF2 and TF3. After the war, Richborough port silted up and the train ferries were laid up until their purchase by Societé Belgo-Anglaise des Ferryboats, (part-owned by the LNER) for the Harwich-Zeebrugge freight service inaugurated in 1926.

The LMS started a short-lived service of passenger ships (not train ferries) between Tilbury and Dunkirk in 1927, in conjunction with the ALA (Angleterre-Lorraine-Alsace SA de Navigation de Dunkerque). This service proved unreliable because of the prevalence of fog in the Thames Estuary.

Fifty years later, it is interesting to reflect that the impetus to Sir Herbert Walker's enthusiasm for a

THE NIGHT FERRY

passenger and freight cross-Channel ferry service was a result of the British Parliament's free vote rejecting proposals for a Channel Tunnel in 1930. Plans for train ferry operation were formulated immediately.

In 1932 the ALA ships were transferred to Folkestone to continue a Dunkirk service from that port. The following year the SR obtained control of the ALA, although the company still existed. The three ships continued to run the Folkestone-Dunkirk service until 1936, when they were sold to shipbreakers, all being second-hand LMS West Coast steamers.

Storm damage caused serious delays to the opening of the train ferry dock at Dover; the ALA constructed a similar dock at Dunkirk.

Above: An interesting view of 'The Night Ferry' inauguration ceremony, performed at Dover on October 12 1936, by Monsieur Corbin, the French Ambassador to Britain. Reboilered Stirling Class R1 0-6-0T No. 1337 is pictured with one of the high-visibility brake vans specially built for the purpose of manoeuvring rolling stock on and off the ferries. On completion of the ceremony, the invited guests travelled to Paris for a celebration dinner. All 12 sleeping cars returned to Dover aboard the SS Hampton Ferry and were worked to Victoria in two trains of six cars. Hence, the first public run of 'The Night Ferry' occurred on October 14 1936 from London to Paris, with six sleeping cars. The first public run from Paris was made with the same coaches on the following day.

The choice of Dunkirk for the continental train ferry terminal was dictated by the fact that it already had a lock and was not therefore subject to tidal influence. These tidal concerns were the reason for the expensive construction of the enclosed dock at Dover, a difficult task that took three years. The three ships required, *Twickenham Ferry, Hampton Ferry* and *Shepperton*

Right: An unidentified guest watches the French stevedores at work at Dunkirk, on October 13 1936, the inaugural return trip of the new service. After being shunted on to the train deck, the cars were jacked up to take the weight off the springs, then they were securely chained to purpose-built heavy hooks beside the adjacent track. The aim of the 'Night Ferry' was not to provide faster transport between the English and French capitals, rather a comfortable night service which enabled the passenger to take to his berth in London, and wake up in France with sufficient time to enjoy breakfast and arrive in Paris in time to start work.

Left: The works at Dover on the train ferry terminal still appear to be incomplete (probably as a consequence of the problems encountered in construction of the purpose-built dock) as Class 0-6-0 No. 1722 and Class H 0-4-4T No. 1530 stand ready to haul two rakes of sleeping cars off the *Hampton Ferry* , following the inaugural run, on October 13 1936. The public trains left London Victoria at 22.00 and Paris Nord at 21.50, each service taking nearly 11 hours, the Channel crossing taking 4 1/4 hours.

Ferry were built at Swan Hunter's Tyneside yard in 1934-5 and subsequently laid up at Southampton pending completion of the works at Dover.

In September 1936, ownership of the *Twickenham Ferry* was transferred from the SR to the ALA to maintain continued employment for the seamen from the ships about to be displaced from the Folkestone-Dunkirk service.

It had been envisaged that the train ferry service would be inaugurated in the summer of 1935, but the construction problems at Dover delayed services until October 1936. The train ferries had four tracks, each capable of holding three sleeping cars or up to ten wagons, according to length. Above the train deck was a car deck, the ships thereby providing the first Roll-on-Roll-off facility now regarded as normal. The sleep

ing cars were specially built to the British loading gauge for the train's operators, Compagnie Internationale des Wagons Lits et des Grands Express Européens. The war years apart, the blue sleeping cars became a familiar sight in Platform 2 at Victoria each morning on arrival and each evening on departure of the 'Night Ferry'.

The train was eventually withdrawn in 1980 for several reasons. Although further sleeping cars were built in 1952, all but four of the original 1936-vintage cars were still in service and overdue for replacement. The passenger service by this time was making a substantial loss, however. To put the matter in perspective, in the 1930s the Imperial Airways airliners of the Handley Page 42 'Hannibal' class flew from Croydon Airport to Paris with up to 40 passengers at a speed of 100

Above: A meeting of English and French railwaymen at Victoria on October 15 1936, as a Southern Railway porter passes luggage through a carriage window to a CIWL train attendant. The French attendants were specially chosen for their knowledge of English. The Topical Press Agency caption reads: "By this new service, passengers are enabled to board a train in London and journey to Paris without changing."

mph. However, by this stage, the rapid development of the British European Airways fleet of jet aircraft now carried the prestige traffic in greater numbers and at much greater speed. Furthermore, and perhaps more importantly, the ever increasing demands of freight traffic contributed to the demise of the 'Night Ferry' in 1980, eight years after the 'Golden Arrow' was withdrawn. Of the 1936-built 'Night Ferry' cars, CIWL No. 3792 is now preserved by the National Railway Museum, at York.

Chapter 7:
SOUTHAMPTON DOCKS

IN 1892 the LSWR made a very prudent investment when it purchased the Southampton Docks Company. Apart from its own services to Honfleur (withdrawn in 1932), Le Havre and the Channel Islands, the Docks had been used by ocean shipping for many years. The White Star Line moved to Southampton in 1911 to be joined by Cunard nine years later. It will be recalled that the then latest White Star liner, the RMS *Titanic* sailed from Southampton on its fateful maiden voyage in 1912.

The LSWR set in motion a number of improvements, notably the construction of a floating dock to enable repairs to be carried out on liners. Authorised in 1922 and built by Armstrong Whitworth & Co. Ltd., it was opened in the summer of 1924. The LSWR had also given consideration to extending the quays westward along the River Test, towards Millbrook, involving the reclamation of land. This was authorised by the newly-formed SR Board to provide extra quay space. Having reclaimed more than 400

Above: A September 1913 view of the Old Docks at Southampton, with a small Drummond Class K10 4-4-0 in charge of a freight train in the foreground, for the Portsmouth line. This must have been a time exposure, indicated by the blurred engine in the middle distance on the right, which is doubtless one of the outside-cylinder Class B4 0-4-0Ts, powerful for their size, 14 of which were allocated to the Docks at this time. The building on the right, with a private siding, occupied by a coal wagon, is designated LSWR INVOICING OFFICE. Most of the other buildings are warehouses. The long low wooden building in the centre of the view, highlights some features of interest. Just to the left, above the rear of the Portsmouth goods train is a stationary Class B4 0-4-0T. To the right of the the same building is a repainted LSWR open goods wagon (N0. 6037) and two double bolster wagons each loaded with two tarpaulin-covered LSWR horse drays. Many more similar loads can be seen in the sidings to the left of and behind the same building.

Above: This impressive view was taken from the top of the dock's massive 150-ton capacity floating crane. Apart from its duties around the docks, it was also used in the loading, transportation and unloading of locomotives and rolling stock between the mainland and the Isle of Wight. The most famous vessel here is Cunard's *Berengaria* (on the right) which was built in 1913 as the SS *Imperator* for the Hamburg Amerika Line, and ceded to Great Britain in 1919 as part of the war reparations. Several Cunard ships had been torpedoed and sunk in the Atlantic Ocean, notably the *Lusitania,* a sister ship of the *Mauretania.* SS *Imperator* (renamed *Berengaria* in April 1921) was one of three large liners built for the Hamburg Amerika Line, although the third (the *Bismark*) was far from complete in 1914 and when she eventually was finished became White Star Line's *Majestic.* The other member of the trio ultimately became the United States Line's *Leviathan.* All were of course very familiar at Southampton in the 1920s and 1930s. *Berengaria* served on the North Atlantic service during the 1920s, and cruises during the 1930s; she was withdrawn and sold for scrap in 1938, but the Second World War postponed her fate, breaking-up not being completed until 1946. At left in dock undergoing its first overhaul there, in this January 1933 picture, is the Canadian Pacific Steamhips Ltd vessel SS *Duchess of Richmond*, then four years old, and hitherto based at Liverpool. Liners were so dealt with in slack periods - thus in the winter of 1933-4 nine liners were overhauled.

acres of mudland, the SR encouraged the development of a large industrial estate. To this day the main road in the New Docks area is named Sir Herbert Walker Avenue after the LSWR's last and the SR's first General Manager, whose far-sightedness conceived this plan. The main quay, 7,500ft in length, could accommodate eight ocean liners. In 1930, at a time of industrial depression and with some Government assistance, the SR started construction of the world's largest graving dock, large enough to accommodate Cunard's proposed new liner, ultimately to become the RMS *Queen Mary.*

Using 750,000 tons of concrete and costing nearly £2 million, this dock was completed in 2 1/2 years and opened by HM King George V in 1933. By this time the world's major shipping lines were attracted to Southampton Docks, with its excellent facilities. The arrival and departure of each liner would lead to the running of several Ocean Liner spe-cials to or from Waterloo. As late as 1950, BR had sufficient faith in the future of liner travel to open a new Ocean Terminal at Southampton Docks. The famous Cunard liner RMS *Queen Mary* was the largest vessel to use the docks in the 1930s, with the ability to carry 2,139 passengers, looked after by no fewer than 1,101 crew members. She was joined by RMS *Queen Elizabeth* after the Second World War, during which both vessels carried out trooping duties. As the North Atlantic passengers progressively transferred to air travel the 'Queens' were used, less than successfully, on winter cruising. In 1966, a six-weeks seaman's strike did further harm. They departed from Southampton for the last time in 1967, by which time the cross-Channel sailings to Le Havre and those to the Channel Islands had forsaken Southampton too.

At the last pre-war Annual General Meeting of the SR, in February 1939, the Chairman remarked that the previous year had seen the celebration of the centenary of Southampton Docks. Commenting on the tremendous progress made since, he noted that Southampton was the premier passenger port in the country, dealing with 47% of its passenger traffic, the next highest handling only 18% of the national total. As a cargo port it ranked fourth in national importance, with a total import and export trade valued at nearly £74 million. International tension had reduced these figures somewhat. Sadly, the Chairman's expression of hope that the troubled period was over was not to be realised, for war broke out with Germany on September 3 1939, after a summer of increasing international tension.

The figures quoted show that although the glamour of the Docks tended to be focussed on the luxurious passenger liners (to view which the SR ran regular excursions), there was nevertheless significant cargo trade. Inevitably,

Southampton was a target during the war and the Docks and town sustained a great deal of damage. In spite of this, the Docks had played key role in the D-Day landings and subsequent traffic. Much of the pre-fabricated port known as 'Mulberry Harbour,' used at Arromanches, Normandy, was constructed in and around Southampton. Perhaps the most significant statistics available are that by VE Day more than 3,500,000 Allied troops had sailed from Southampton and the military stores tonnage handled in the 17 weeks after D-Day equalled the Docks combined import/exchange tonnage for the whole of 1938.

While the passenger liners had the unfortunate habit, from the operational point of view, of arriving or departing in groups in a single day, the cargo traffic was there to be handled every day of the year. After recovery from the immediate after-effects of the war, the Docks handled some 300,000 passengers a year and one million bags of mail, while freight traffic required 120,000 wagons in each direction, inwards and outwards. There were 78 miles of railway tracks in the Docks, requiring an allocation of 19 shunting locomotives, relying on hand signalling only. There were more than 100 operating staff and latterly the locomotives were equipped with two-way radios. Construction of the New Docks in the 1930s was a great act of faith by the SR and one of its outstanding achievements. In the totally changed shipping scene of the 1980s, Southampton handles significant amounts of container traffic west of the former New Docks area. The King George V Graving Dock is used occasionally, though for ships much smaller than those for which it was designed.

Above: A June 1928 view of the old docks. In the foreground are Cunard's *Mauretania*, with White Star Line's SS *Olympic* adjacent in Berth No. 47, from which its ill-fated sister ship RMS *Titanic* sailed in 1912. Five other liners are also berthed. When Cunard and White Star Lines (eventually to merge in 1934) deserted Liverpool for Southampton in 1911 (White Star) and 1920 (Cunard) some of the tugs of the Alexandra Towing Company transferred with them to continue their long association with the liner companies. SS *Olympic* appears ready to sail, as tugs are stationed fore and aft to assist her into the Solent. Note the intricate network of dockside railways.

Left: Eight liners are pictured in this mid-1930s aerial view of the docks. In order of size these were: SS *Majestic* (White Star), SS *Berengaria* (Cunard), SS *Olympic* (White Star), SS *Empress of Britain* (Canadian Pacific Steamships), SS *Homeric* (White Star), SS *Asturias* (Royal Mail Lines) SS *Warwick Castle* (Union Castle) SS *Orontes* (Orient Line). The view is looking towards the Solent Estuary. White Star's SS *Homeric* in the foreground is in the floating dock. The white-towered building - still there in the 1980s - is the Royal Pier used by Red Funnel ships then, as now, on their Isle of Wight service

Below: His Majesty King George V opened the 1,200ft Graving Dock that was to bear his name on July 26 1933. The dock was at the northern end of the New Docks. It has been suggested that Sir Herbert Walker was less than enthusiastic about the graving dock, as it would see only occasional use, and which was primarily intended for the RMS *Queen Mary*, at that time still under construction and un-named. Cunard Chairman Sir Percy Bates, said that the new ship would be based at Liverpool if the new dock was not built and this threat saved the day for Southampton. On January 19 1934, five Alexandra tugs manoeuvred the *Majestic* into the dock. With an overall length of 956ft and gross tonnage of 56,551, she was then the world's largest liner. Four pumps, each handling more than 1,000 gallons per minute, emptied the 263,000-gallon dock in less than four hours. The ship is dressed overall for the occasion; the world's largest liner in the world's biggest graving dock.

Left: One or more Ocean Liner Specials would be run by the SR for each liner arrival or departure. Here, on May 27 1936, 'Lord Nelson' 4-6-0 No. 852 *Sir Walter Raleigh* arrives in the docks with a Pullman special for the maiden voyage of the RMS *Queen Mary*. Pullman cars were not provided on Ocean Liner Specials until 1931, the cars for the service mostly being transferred to the SR from the GWR, which had an uneasy association with the Pullman Car Company in 1929/30 for its Plymouth liner specials (many of the liners being diverted to Southampton on opening of the New Docks) and the 'Torbay Pullman.' The Pullmans had been deeply resented by the GWR dining car staff. Trains formed entirely of Pullman cars ran only for the largest liners and only certain trains included Pullman cars. Much depended on the size and prestige of the ship. Thus, in 1938 a train serving the flagship of the French fleet (CGT) the SS *Normandie*, consisted of six Pullman cars, five SR corridor coaches and three vans.

Facing Page: Until construction of the New Docks, in the 1930s, which together with the older facilities provided berthing accommodation for 20 liners, many foreign-flagged liners did not venture beyond Southampton Water, their passengers embarking or disembarking by tender. The first German vessel to sail from the Docks with passengers in post-war years was the SS *Bremen*, of the North German Lloyd Line, at New Docks Berth No. 101, in May 1933. This vessel had in fact also used the Floating Dock before its maiden voyage, in July 1929. White Star's SS *Homeric* had been the first vessel to use the New Docks in December 1932. Much still had to be done to complete the extension at this time, but this June 1937 picture portrays the greater part of the New Docks in final form. The Graving Dock alongside the River Test cannot be seen but was to the right of this viewpoint. One of the SR ships is in dry dock at centre right. The large white building in the foreground is a cold storage warehouse. All the aerial photographs in this chapter were probably taken from aircraft flying from Southampton's Eastleigh Airport.

Right: After the Second World War, in 1946/47, the LSWR Class B4 0-4-0Ts formerly used on the dock railways were replaced by surplus American-built US Transportation Corps 0-6-0Ts. This December 6 1955 photograph shows the radio telephones fitted to the docks locomotives, to assist shunting. This radio link between the controllers and footplatemen accelerated operations considerably, for previously messages had ben conveyed on foot to engine crews. Driver Albert Russell, a 55 years old footplatemen of 36 years service, uses the radio to receive instructions whilst waiting to shunt 45 wagons; he is accompanied by Fireman David Neil.

IT tends to be overlooked in these days, when BR has shed all but its most profitable bulk freight traffic, that the railways used to be regarded as common carriers; they were expected to accept any freight offered (subject to loading gauge restrictions) at a fixed charge, according to the classification of merchandise. Therefore, virtually every station on the SR had a goods yard, to which a daily pick-up goods train ran; it was so called but it also set down wagons. There were more than 700 such yards at Nationalisation, but in the next 15 years or so they were progressively closed.

The wagon loads arrived and were despatched from a main sorting siding, where they were made into trainloads according to their destination. Sorting sidings, later to be known as marshalling yards, were mostly level, but as early as 1882 when the LNWR completed its yard at Edge Hill, Liverpool, gravity shunting was used.

The principal use of this type of shunting on the SR was at the LSWR's Feltham yard, constructed in the early 1920s. The railway was expected to carry coal, cement, ship masts (on bolster wagons) electric generators as out-of-gauge loads, for which special arrangements had to be made. Livestock, cattle, sheep, day-old chicks and pedigree racehorses were also carried by rail.

After the First World War, a transport revolution took place. The War Office had large numbers of surplus lorries for disposal and these were eagerly bought, often by former servicemen familiar with these vehicles, and they became road haulage carriers, perhaps in their own districts, but able to pick and choose what loads they could carry. As motor lorries increased in size and became more reliable, railway freight receipts were seriously affected. Freight handling was labour intensive, and until remarkably late in years, often horsedrawn. Indeed, horses tended to

Right: Holly is unloaded from a box van at Nine Elms, in December 1922. Whilst hardly a heavy commodity for the railways to handle, this must certainly have been one of the most awkward! Presumably it is the 'Gaffer' in the bowler hat.

Chapter 8:
GOODS TRAFFIC

Above: Horse-drawn wagons, their charges having departed, are unloaded in the Stores Department at Nine Elms, in July 1917. A far cry indeed from the block load traffic of today.

Left: Another December 1922 scene at the SR's Nine Elms Goods Depot, depicting the Christmas rush. In this view, numerous crates of bacon are awaiting despatch, each bearing the notice that: "Davies Bacon is cured for immediate consumption." In the distance can be seen an asssortment of motor and horse-drawn road delivery vehicles.

Below: The SR was one of three of the main line companies to have a joint interest in the West London line and here at Kensington, a pair of gleaming Humber cars are being carefully handled by railwaymen (below, right) in October 1932, in connection with the Motor Show at Olympia. One wonders what the delightful MG open sports car (below, left) would be worth nowadays?

stay later in large towns, where stable accommodation and veterinary attention was available, while the lorries went to country districts, where they could cover a wide area.

In 1938, by which time the SR's motor vehicle total was rapidly catching up, there were still 200 more horse-drawn carts than motor vehicles. The war years from 1939 to 1945 slowed the decline of the railway horse, which was sometimes also used for shunting wagons in busy yards, but from 1930 the introduction of tractors, known as 'mechanical horses' with automatic couplings to join or separate from their trailers began the great decline of the railway horse.

In post-war years, these gradually gave way to orthodox lorries. With the departure of the last railway horse in 1967 (at Newmarket) and bearing in mind that it had not only been the railways that had once relied entirely on horse-drawn vehicles, a once lucrative traffic was lost - manure, conveyed in open wagons to country stations for agricultural purposes!

Road competition really began to hit hard in the 1930s and in 1938 the railways joined together in appealing for a Square Deal. The problem was that the road haulier could be selective in carrying only the most profitable commodities, paid only the vehicle licence and petrol tax and often tended to ignore vehicle weight limits or drivers working hours. The railways, on the other hand, had to charge substantial rates and were unable to compete on equal terms - they could not, for example, increase their rates

Above: By far the best-known Circus in pre-war days was that of the great showman Bertram Mills. This picture was taken at Ascot West on January 26 1933, after a successful Christmas season at Olympia, Kensington. LSWR Drummond 0-6-0 No. 346 stands at the head of a train, led by a typical SECR birdcage roof Guard's Brake followed by a large number of horse boxes. The goods platform here was no doubt specifically designed for horse box traffic, in connection with the adjacent race course. In the background on the far siding, the two nearest vans of SR design were known as Scenery Vans.

Above: The original caption to this January 26 1933 picture reads: 'Mr Bertram Mills famous circus left Kensington this morning to tour the country once again after a successful season at the Olympia, London. A tight fit - the cricketing elephant bends to emerge from his truck on arrival at Ascot West.' The van is one of the Scenery Vans seen in the previous picture.

for carrying loads that road hauliers did not want without adversely affecting British industry as a whole. As common carriers, they had to accept and transport anything that was offered to them. *The 'Daily Telegraph'*, not always known for a sympathetic attitude to the railways, noted at the time:

"With the demand for parity with the road hauliers there can be no quarrel in principle, for it is beyond doubt that the unilateral restriction upon the freedom of the railways in fixing their charges operates unfairly in favour of the road hauliers. It is of the first importance to realise that the railways perform an indispensable function, and that the community therefore has the inescapable obligation of ensuring such conditions as will enable them to pay their way"

There was hope of some degree of control and legislation but all this fell by the wayside on the outbreak of war in September 1939. Nationalisation, which initially included major road haulage companies, which were later privatised, only further aggravated a situation that had become increasingly difficult 20 years earlier. It is a problem which has caused the railways intense difficulties ever since.

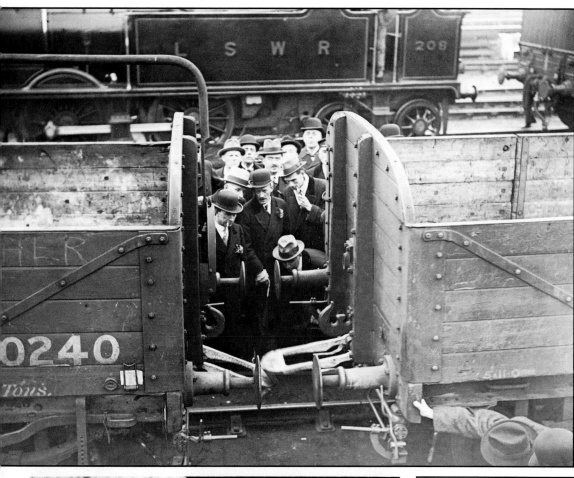

Left & below: Tests regularly took place to improve safety conditions in busy goods yard and this March 1921 view shows the trials of the W.G. Boonzaier automatic coupling, as fitted to a pair of LSWR wagons, at Clapham Junction in March 1921. The new coupling was fitted in addition to standard drawgear, which would be required until such time as the Boonzaier coupling became standard. The operating gear adjacent to the buffers looks rather flimsy and unlikely to stand up to rough shunting. The LSWR Class 02 0-4-4T in the background was sent to the Isle of Wight in 1930 as No. W17 *Seaview*, a sister engine to No. W24 *Calbourne* preserved in running order at the Isle of Wight Steam Centre at Haven Street. This engine, formerly LSWR No. 209, had arrived on the Isle of Wight in 1925.

Left: A passenger examines a Square Deal leaflet at Waterloo in 1937, when the main line companies mounted a joint campaign for fairer goods dealing terms, in the face of competition from road transport. The private lorry was making serious inroads as it could provide a door to door service without loading and unloading en route. At this time, even though the SR did have more than 700 motor lorries, it still retained nearly as many horse-drawn vehicles. The railway companies jointly sought Government aid in the removal of restrictions on rail charges, with the exceptions of iron and steel. The 'Clear the Lines' booklet shown here was produced to enlist passenger support.

FELTHAM YARD

Right: Work proceeding on the construction of Feltham Marshalling Yard in October 1920. The building taking shape on the right is the Up Side Hump Signal Box, controlling only points to the marshalling sidings. In the event of an emergency, the Foreman near the hump summit would be able to throw a signal lever to danger independently of the signalman. In addition, an audible siren would draw the driver's attention to any change in the signal's position. In the centre distance, the main office building is under construction.

Above: During the First World War, large numbers of Great Central Railway Robinson 2-8-0s were built for overseas service, with the Railway Operating Division of the army. Some were built after the Armistice and either stored or loaned to the railway companies. The LSWR, with its lines to Southampton being extremely busy during the war years, faced an acute shortage of serviceable locomotives after the war and several 2-8-0s were loaned to the company for up to a year from the end of 1919. They were eventually released by the entry into traffic of new Urie Class S15 4-6-0s. This immaculate ROD 2-8-0 is standing in the incomplete Feltham Yard in October 1920, bearing headcode discs for a transfer freight to Willesden LNWR.

EVEN after the LSWR Locomotive Works was moved from Nine Elms to Eastleigh by 1911, the sorting of freight wagons in the inadequate space of the sidings at Nine Elms was ineffective and led to delays. It soon became clear that a new approach to the problem must be made. Sir Herbert Walker, the LSWR General Manager, had seen gravity shunting carried out in marshalling yards in the USA and decided that he must identify a suitable open site, for such a yard, easy of access not only to LSWR trains, but also to those of the northern companies. A 79-acre site was chosen at Feltham, hitherto agricultural land. At the time, this was a departure from the previous practice of extending existing yards, often in built-up areas, with space constraints.

Feltham was easy of access to the North & South West Junction line used by trains to and from the GCR at Neasden and also the Midland Railway at Cricklewood, while the North London line from Willesden Junction gave access to GER trains from Stratford. Willesden LNWR and Old Oak Common GWR were reached via Clapham Junction and the West London Railway and its Extension. A bonus was the fact that the new yard would be situated outside the increasingly busy suburban electrified area. Equally, the LSWR's own traffic from the main lines ran to and from Feltham by means of loop lines to the east of Farnborough or Byfleet, thereby keeping freight traffic segregated from the busier lines towards London. In any case, by the time the yard was being planned, the line from Waterloo through Basingstoke as far as Worting Junction had been quadrupled, this being the point at which the Southampton and Salisbury lines diverged.

By the spring of 1918 the work was well in hand with the LSWR's Engineers Department staff augmented in the initial stages by 200 German prisoners of war. Three years later construction was well advanced, the gravity humps commencing operation on May 1 1921, initially using loaned ROD 2-8-0s of GCR design, soon replaced by four purpose-built 4-8-0Ts. In 1923, the sidings were virtually complete and it was intended that there should be eight reception roads and provision for up to 18 marshalling sidings on both up and down sides of the main line. Between reception and marshalling areas the lines converged into a single track where the 7ft 3in gravity humps were situated, each with its adjacent power-operated signal box. In this electronic age we would probably regard the method of operation as both basic and also

Left: Another October 1920 view, showing part of the Feltham Down Yard, with further evidence of the LSWR's locomotive shortage. In the early summer of 1919, the company borrowed seven GNR Class J5 Stirling/Ivatt 0-6-0s (later to become LNER Class J4) built between 1876 and 1900. All were allocated to Strawberry Hill and used for local freight trips or yard shunting. Two of these are seen shunting at Feltham, the leading vehicle of the right hand train being a cattle wagon washed out with lime after its last occupants had left. When built, Feltham yard was provided with cattle pens. The GNR 0-6-0s started to drift back to Doncaster soon after, although their return was phased over a few months. Three MR Kirtley 0-6-0s of 1872 vintage were also loaned to Guildford at this time to help during the engine shortage.

Above: Because of the cross-Channel links, SR officials always maintained close contact with their French counterparts. In this May 1929 view, a group of French railway officials is being shown round the yard at Feltham. They are standing beside the Down Hump Signal Box, beside one of the massive Urie Class H16 4-8-0T hump shunting engines. On the left are the wagon repair shops whilst on the right can be seen the mechanical coaling plant of the new locomotive depot.

rather labour intensive.

As trains came into the reception sidings, the train engine was detached and proceeded to go to the neighbouring engine shed. Then, one of the big eight-coupled tanks would come on the rear and propel the train at less than walking pace to the hump, where it came under the supervision of a yard foreman and a head shunter. One would identify the destinations from the wagon labels, the other would chalk the appropriate siding number on each rake of wagons and the signalman set the points accordingly. The gradients were 1 in 60 up to each hump and 1 in 50 down in each case for a distance of about 200 ft. Three more shunters were needed to apply the brakes on each rake of wagons to bring them to rest in the appropriate place. Each day the yard handled 2,500 wagons, more or less equally divided between the up and down humps.It was reckoned that a 70-wagon train could be divided into more than 50 rafts of wagons in 12 minutes. The lighting was adequate for the work to be carried out as quickly after dark as it

was during daylight.

Each marshalling siding represented a particular destination; for example, apart from traffic within the LSWR system on the up side, there were individual sidings for wagons to the GCR, GNR, LNWR, Midland and North London Railways. On the down side all sidings were for destinations on the LSWR system, although some wagons could have been bound ultimately for GWR destinations, via Basingstoke or Salisbury, so giving the LSWR maximum revenue.

The total yard capacity was 3,500 wagons and a repair shop was provided for attention to crippled wagons. In addition, provision was made for an engine shed, construction of which did not commence until 1923. In the meantime, engines ran to and from the shed at Strawberry Hill, near Twickenham. As this shed was being run-down in its use by steam engines, so it was progressively converted to become an EMU depot, in which form it is still in use. The Feltham shed, fully operational by 1924, was built in pre-cast concrete and set the

pattern for other steam sheds built or rebuilt in SR days. It provided covered accommodation for about 40 tender engines, with a 65 ft turntable and a mechanical coaling plant. By 1937 it had an allocation of 70 engines but its strategic importance in the subsequent war led to an increase of this number by 25.

For long distance freight (and occasional summer passenger use) the 20 engines of the rugged Urie Class S15 4-6-0 introduced in 1920 were allocated there in 1947, as were many of the Maunsell engines of the same class. For transfer freight work, Urie built five handsome 4-6-2Ts, which in SR days were painted in the green passenger livery and could also be seen on Ascot race specials or Waterloo empty stock trains. By the 1960s, there was a considerable reduction in the use of the yard and the 4-6-0s and large tank engines were all withdrawn before the end of 1965. Two years later the shed closed for steam engines. A small shed was erected for use by diesel engines but this too had closed by 1970 and now the yard is but a memory.

HITHER GREEN SIDINGS

Right: A familiar sight at this yard was the Wainwright Class C 0-6-0. On November 13 1930 No. 1461 was used in tests with a rail built buffer stop. This buffer was unusual in having two additional rails, each side of the running tracks, attached both to the sleepers and also the buffer. The tracks were loosely connected so that when the train hit the buffers the stop block slid, absorbing the impact to stop the runaway. The locomotive is seen here dragging the buffer stop into its normal position, after an impact test with a 600-ton train running at 8mph.

IN 1898, the SER implemented a plan to streamline goods operations, purchasing initially 21 acres of open land at Hither Green, where extensive sidings were developed. This was well situated to exchange traffic with other railways in the London area, notably via the West London Railway, GWR and LNWR, the Metropolitan Widened Lines, GNR and MR, and the East London Railway and the GER, as well as its southern neighbours. In July 1929, a new loop was opened at Lewisham, using part of the track-

Above: In February 1948, a shunter at Hither Green exchanges a few words with the driver of a Maunsell Class Z 0-8-0T. Only three months later, steam shunting locomotives in this yard were superseded by 350 hp 0-6-0 diesels. The pictures on this page are highly indicative of the imaginativee style and approach of the *Picture Post* photographers; these views being produced as part of a feature entitled *Double Moonlight,* depicting the busy after-dark activity at Hither Green. The Z Class three-cylinder 0-8-0Ts, (BR Nos 30950-30957) were introduced in 1929. By 1959, all eight members of this class were based at Exmouth Junction, where they were used chiefly on banking duties on the steeply-graded line between Exeter Central and Exeter St Davids stations. The class was extinct by the end of 1962, when all eight examples were scrapped. These powerful locomotives, which were given a BR power classification of 6F, weighed more than 71 tons and had a tractive effort of 29,376lbs.

bed of the closed LCDR Greenwich Park branch. This route afforded trains from the Metropolitan Widened Lines an easier connection than that hitherto used over the busy lines through London Bridge from the spur at Metropolitan Junction. From 1933 Hither Green sidings were considerably extended, notably on the down side - there was less room for expansion on the up side.

A new engine shed was opened in September 1933, this also providing much relief for the as then unmodernised shed at Bricklayers Arms. Unlike Feltham, the yard was not mechanised although practices were similar, with gravity shunting employed. As at Norwood Junction, up and down sides were separated by four-track passenger lines which meant that several trip workings were needed between yards each day. These had to be accomplished as quickly as possible, to avoid delays to passenger traffic. At both Feltham and Hither Green the down yard was larger than the up side. By 1934, Hither Green could accommodate 1,210 wagons on 25 roads in the down yard, whereas the up yard capacity was for 600 wagons on ten roads.

Unlike the other main line companies, freight formed only a small percentage of traffic on the SR, which was predominantly a passenger line. No doubt a large proportion of traffic on the up side consisted of returning empty wagons, which required less shunting.

Shunting the yard in early SR days was largely entrusted to reboilered Stirling Class 01 0-6-0s. Based at Orpington shed until that shed closed following electrification, they were then supplied by Bricklayers Arms, until the Hither Green shed was ready, in 1933. The modern LSWR marshalling yard at Feltham used purpose-built 4-8-0Ts, also used on short transfer freights, and more were on order in 1922, but they were thought too large and expensive merely for shunting work and in 1929 Brighton Works built eight Class Z 0-8-0Ts, designed by Maunsell. These three-cylinder engines were fitted with a free-steaming boiler based on a trusted LBSCR design, with a high tractive effort and moderate axle loading. Up to four of these powerful tank engines were normally employed in Hither Green yard and remained so until the spring of 1948 when they were displaced by diesels and transferred elsewhere. The by then elderly Class 01 0-6-0s were still giving a helping hand at this stage, although not on the gravity shunting duties for which the 0-8-0Ts were better-suited.

Left: Also in February 1948, and now employed by British Railways rather than the Southern Railway, the Hither Green wheeltapper goes about his business during a lull in shunting. On today's hi-tech railway, the once-familiar sight and sound of the wheeltapper has given way to the ultrasonic examination.

Chapter 9:
TROUBLED TIMES

SNOW

Above: Heavy snowfall and subsequent flooding caused severe problems on the SR over Christmas 1927, and into the New Year. The most spectacular incident was at Amesbury, Wiltshire, where three LSWR locomotives propelling a snow plough were stranded in a snow drift which was 18ft high in places. A large team of permanent way men had to be called to dig them out. When they eventually reached home on New Years Eve they certainly deserved to sit down and toast in the New Year. The caption mentions to four locomotives but contemporary railway press reports refer only to three, the number seen' here, apparently an Adams Class '0460' 4-4-0. a Drummond Class '700' 0-6-0 and an Adams 'Highflyer' 4-4-0 with 6ft 7in wheels, either Class T3 or X6.

Right: When eventually released, the locomotives appeared to clear the snow to some effect. Amesbury is about midway between Andover and Salisbury on the main line to the west. An after effect of the thaw was a severe landslide in the cutting which blocked Merstham tunnel on the SECR line on the London side of Redhill.

MISHAPS

IT may seem that a disproportionate amount of space has been devoted to accidents, scattered about this book, but they have been chosen to illustrate particular points, for example, the mass of lines radiating from the two London Bridge stations. Furthermore, there is much interest in the causes and effects of accidents. In fact, the Southern Railway, despite its intensive passenger service, had a better safety record than the northern companies, coming second only to the GWR, which although protected by its Automatic Train Control had a less-frequent service of trains. With the appointment of John Elliot as Public Relations Assistant in 1925 - the first PR man in this country - the SR tended to take its own photographs and distribute them to the appropriate newspapers with press releases. Thus, it sometimes took an accident, whether large or small, to prompt an Editor to send a press photographer to the SR. The SR's safety record was so good that only two accidents resulted in passenger fatalities of double figures: Sevenoaks, in 1927, and South Croydon, 20 years later.

The railways are also subject to disruption caused by bad weather, and the photographs illustrating the SR combatting the after-effects of snow come remarkably from the west country, which normally only suffered on very high ground or during serious blizzards. Again, the SR was more fortunate than its northern neighbours in suffering little disruption from snow, with the possible exception of lines in East Kent. After electrification it also suffered from occasional disruption, through ice on conductor rails in hard winters. Up to this time, the SR had to contend with serious autumn and winter fogs notably in suburban areas, and the worst accident in BR days on its lines occurred in dense fog at St Johns, near Lewisham, in 1957, before the Clean Air Act of 1956 started to take effect. That the SR enjoyed such a mishap-free record was tribute indeed to its operating practices and staff.

The SR had to contend with wartime difficulties, and throughout the Second World War the company was in the front line. Of all the country's main line railways, it played the most prominent part in putting on at short notice a remarkable number of extra trains to convey troops from South Coast ports in the successful evacuation of the Dunkirk beaches in 1940, in which SR vessels also took part. Then came the aerial blitz by the Luftwaffe and later the V1 flying bombs and V2 rockets, all of which

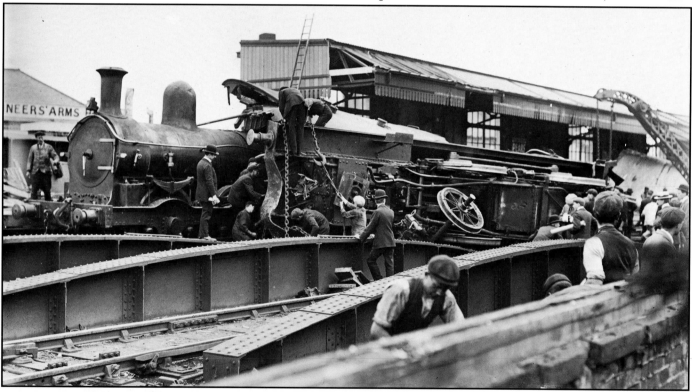

Above: At the height of the rivalry between the GWR (which carried the mails) and LSWR (carrying the passengers) over the Plymouth Ocean Liner service, the element of racing between the two companies - in the course of which GWR 4-4-0 *City of Truro* was said to have attained over 100 mph on Wellington bank in May 1904 - was brought to a disastrous close when the LSWR express conveying passengers from the liner *New York* was derailed at Salisbury on July 1 1906. These were the only trains not scheduled to stop at Salisbury and the locomotive change took place at Templecombe, where the train was on time that night. Because of the urge to run fast with these lightly-loaded trains, Drummond had given strict instructions to all drivers not to run ahead of time. From that day to this it is totally inexplicable why the driver of Class L12 4-4-0 No. 421 should have approached Salisbury West at double the speed restriction of 30 mph. No 421 appears to have tilted over and hit an incoming train of milk empties, becoming derailed and colliding with No. 0351, a Beyer Peacock 0-6-0. This, the worst disaster on the LSWR, involved the death of 24 passengers and four railwaymen. In view of the complete destruction of the train it is remarkable that 19 passengers survived.

Above: On August 29 1912, the nine coach 6.37pm Aldershot-Waterloo headed by an 0-4-4T was standing in the up through road at Vauxhall, when it was run into by 'T9' 4-4-0 No. 312 running tender-first, light engine from Nine Elms to Waterloo. The tender bore the brunt of the damage although several carriages suffered severely, including Third Brake No. 1519 which was destroyed. One passenger was killed. The light engine driver was confused as to which track he was occupying and passed the up through line signal at danger. This clearly shows a Drummond 'T9' in original condition before the fitting of a superheated boiler.

wrought havoc on SR lines. Most noteworthy amongst the SR's wide-ranging contribution to the war effort was the dedicated toil of those responsible for getting the lines cleared after enemy action, to restore the train service. All the major termini suffered to a greater or lesser degree, and Ashford Works was only a few minutes flying time from the airfields in occupied France. Inevitably, therefore, it suffered 3,000 air raid

Above: A remarkable head-on collision between two goods trains, one about to enter Hither Green sidings, the other about to leave. The engines involved were Wainwright Class C 0-6-0 No. 1691 (on the train in the foreground) and LNER Class N1 0-6-2T No 4561 on the train about to leave for Ferme Park sidings, Hornsey, via the 1929 spur line at Lewisham, Snow Hill tunnel, Holborn and the Metropolitan 'Widened Lines.' Note the then relatively new container

wagons behind the leading brake van of the SR train, in which a number of wagons have telescoped. The accident occurred on September 4 1934 and in the background can be seen the new Hither Green engine shed, opened on September 10 1933. This depot not only served the extensive sidings, but it also eased the load on the old engine shed at Bricklayers Arms, later to be partly rebuilt. Note the extensive telescoping of No. 4561's train, on the extreme right.

warnings and some direct hits, nevertheless the works staff were not diverted from their job of building locomotives and wagons for the war effort. A notable order was for 1,000 open wagons urgently needed for the USSR, completed within ten weeks and delivered via the Middle East. In addition to maintaining and building locomotives and rolling stock, the SR works at Ashford, Brighton, Eastleigh and Lancing were actively engaged on vital war work. In view of the important part played by Hampshire and Southampton in particular in the 1944 invasion of occupied France, it was appropriate that among other vital war work Eastleigh was chosen to build motor landing craft. In the build up to D Day and its aftermath, an enormous number of men and materials had to be carried to the Hampshire area and since the traditional Channel ports were too close to France, it was the Southern Railway's Southampton Docks that bore the brunt. Particularly remarkable is that in the four months following D Day, the amount of military tonnage handled equalled the total imports and exports of the peak year of 1938. As soon as Cherbourg was liberated, SR train ferries *Hampton Ferry* and *Twickenham Ferry* were in daily use, carrying British War Department and USA Transportation Corps locomotives, ambulance trains and rolling stock across the Channel to relieve the beleaguered European railways, many of whose locomotives and stock had been impounded and taken to Germany. SR ships too were involved in the D Day landings and ensuing troop movements, while other vessels were used as hospital ships or minesweepers.

Left, above: On June 28 1937 the late-running 8.17pm Margate-Victoria (via Maidstone East) train passed Swanley Junction home signal at speed and instead of running through the up main platform, was diverted into a short siding, demolishing a wagon and two LBSCR carriages and damaging the electrical switching station. Four passengers were killed, but the crew of Class L 4-4-0 No. 1768 escaped serious injury. At the time, the station was as built, with separate platforms serving each of the two routes (see also page 17) but two years later the present station, north of the junction was opened. The junction distant signal was moved further from the home signal to allow adequate time for braking.

Left, lower: The aftermath of the mishap near Catford on September 20 1946, when 'Schools' 4-4-0 No. 917 *Ardingly* was derailed and its train ran down the embankment. Fortunately, no great speed was involved and No. 917 remained on the trackbed; there was only one fatality, sadly, an RAF Flying Officer who had survived the war. A corridor coach and four coaches of 1925-built set 460 were destroyed. The train was the 2.10pm Victoria-Ramsgate and the mishap was caused by wartime arrears of track maintenance.

Right: The worst accident ever to take place on the SR occurred in thick fog between Purley Oaks and South Croydon on October 24 1947, when the 8.4am Tattenham Corner--London Bridge train ran into the rear of the 7.33am service from Haywards Heath to London Bridge, which was just moving off from a signal check. Thirty one passengers and a motorman were killed. An inexperienced signalman admitted that he had forgotten the Haywards Heath train was in his section and, thinking a signal failure had occurred, he used the releasing key of the Sykes block system, enabling him irregularly to give a clear signal to the Tattenham Corner train. Four carriages were destroyed. Buses can be seen in this view of the wreckage, waiting to carry away uninjured passengers.

WARTIME: 1939 - 1945

Right: Although fortunately never needed, gas masks had to be carried at all times during the Second World War, and this picture was taken at Waterloo in June 1939 to illustrate how railwaymen would be expected to conform to this ruling. Heavy gloves are also being worn by this engine crew, who would in reality have probably found it very difficult to perform out their duties. The SR staff were certainly in the front line during the war. Even before war broke out on September 3 1939, locomotives were fitted with Air Raid Precaution guard rails to carry a tarpaulin blackout sheet between the cab roof and the front of the tender, to conceal as far as possible the glare of the fire from enemy aircraft seeking their targets. The locomotive is 'King Arthur' 4-6-0 No. 779 *Sir Colgrevance.*

This page: These pictures were taken in November 1943 to illustrate how the SR was ready for gas attacks. The original Topical Press Agency caption reads: "GAS ON THE RAILWAYS: A big demonstration and exercise open to the railwaymen of Kent areas was given by the Southern Railway recently in the Kent area. For the purpose of the exercise lengths of rails were taken up, a crater dug and mustard gas sprayed in the area. The whole system of gas detection, decontaminating, filling in the crater, fixing and levelling the track and signal and telegraph departments went into action and in a very short space of time the trains moved over the section again."

Left: An overall view of the area of the simulated attack, showing the crater, damaged track and contaminated ground.

Below, left: Wearing full protective clothing, the liquid gas is destroyed by bleach-pasting the whole rail.

Below, right: After completing their decontamination duties, the railwaymen themselves are decontaminated. Pictures like this were judged to be very useful in upholding public morale by demonstrating that all eventualities were being taken into consideration.

Above, left: It is December 1939 and a crowd of evacuated children at Yeovil Town run along the platform to meet parents, relatives and friends who had travelled down to see them by the first cheap-rate excursions operated for this purpose. The engine is a Class U 2-6-0, probably a converted 'River' 2-6-4T, of which several were based at Yeovil.

Above, right: The evacuation of school children and some adults was a priority task. As early as April 1939, special traffic notices were issued from Waterloo to all Sections of the SR. It was then envisaged that nearly 500,000 passengers, mostly children, would be carried from 53 London and suburban stations to 78 destinations in the country or seaside, all this not being expected to interfere with the railways' normal morning and evening business traffic. The plan involved 717 trains, 261 steam and 456 electric. It came into operation on September 1 without a hitch. In the event. only 220,000 passengers were carried, but additionally, 264 trains were provided for the evacuation of the Medway towns and the Portsmouth area, in view of the importance of the naval dockyards. Most of the children seem happy enough, in June 1940, but the teacher seems less certain, whilst the little boy to the left of the door seems especially sad. Note the SR practice of painting the compartment seat numbers on the outside above the windows, to assist those with reserved seats, a practice greatly encouraged by the SR, so that it could have some guide as to how many trains it needed to run on peak Saturdays.

Right: In June 1940, it seems that cricket is to play an important part in their life as evacuees, as these children chat with the engine crew of Urie Class N15 4-6-0 No. 736 *Excalibur*, which was incorporated into the 'King Arthur' class. The engine is painted in an earlier olive green Bulleid livery, tried before malachite green was adopted. However, with the advent of the war all locomotives were painted black.

Left: At the time of this picture, April 22 1941, it was said that 3,200 women had joined SR service as clerks, porters, van girls, stores-women and painters. All were issued with blue serge uniforms. Seven of these ladies are pictured on the Low Level platform at London Bridge. The high level lines to Cannon Street and Charing Cross can be seen on the right. In 1939, the SR had less than 2,000 women employees; by the end of the war this figure had increased to 9,000, while nearly 4,000 men worked on beyond their retirement age. At this time, more than 11,000 company servants were with the military services, and 387 were killed on active service, a further 170 being killed by enemy action whilst on duty. As railwaymen were demobilised, so the women left the SR's payroll.

Above: Also on April 22 1941, the newly-appointed railway women demonstrate that their work required strength and stamina, as they handle mail at London Bridge. The down train (above, left) is headed by a Class L 4-4-0.

Left: Hard luck for a group of commuters in November 1940. There has been an air raid incident, the electric current has been switched off and they have had to alight from their trains and walk, probably in the Lewisham area, although for security reasons this was not disclosed. All being well, they may eventually have been able to board a bus or tram, assuming the roads had not been adversely affected by enemy action.

TROOP TRAIN

THE weekly magazine *Picture Post*, killed off in 1957, chiefly by the growth of instant news on television, specialised in pictorial journalism. These photographs were part of a feature entitled *Troop Train*, depicting a train from 'somewhere in England', actually to Clapham Junction and thence to Southampton Docks, in August 1944.

Right: The engine crew cross the tracks at Clapham Junction in readiness to take charge of 'King Arthur' Class 4-6-0 No. 788 *Sir Urre of the Mount*. SR engines carried headcode discs in daytime, one of which would record the engine's rostered diagram number for its specific working. In this case it is Nine Elms Special Duty No. 3.

Above, left: The driver attends to the lubrication of No 788 in readiness for the arrival of the troop train, doubtless from the West London line, which connected Clapham Junction with some of the Northern companies and also the GWR.

Above, right: At work in the cab of No. 788, which as BR No. 30788 survived until February 1962; the locomotive was scrapped at Ashford Works before the end of the month.

Left: A couple of smiling GIs exchange a friendly word or two with the engine crew, prior to departure for Southampton. Although this picture was without doubt carefully staged by the photographer, it has certainly created an evocative image of the SR at war. Even so, these pictures were not published at the time, for the original *Picture Post* prints are marked 'story killed.'

Above, left: Nearly ready to go, the guard advises the driver of the number of coaches and the tare weight of the train, prior to departure for Southampton. This picture shows the countershaded style of lettering used by the SR for its locomotive numerals at this time.

Above, right: On the road. The driver can be seen on the extreme right as the fireman sets to work with the shovel. This picture once again illustrates the enterprise and initiative of the *Picture Post* photographers, for this cannot have been an easy photograph to take on a fast moving locomotive. Note the cigarette, tucked behind the fireman's ear!

Chapter 10:

MISCELLANY

MOTOR VEHICLES

Below, left: Karrier Motors Ltd of Huddersfield, known as Clayton & Co (Huddersfield) Ltd from its inception in 1904 until 1920, proved a popular choice of sturdy road motor vehicles to the railway companies. As early as 1911 the company was supplying vans to the GCR, LNWR and LSWR. The earliest Karrier 16hp one-ton vans delivered to the LSWR were employed in the Bournemouth district. Van No. 49M, pictured here on show at Manchester, on January 30 1914, was a 25hp two-ton van of which the LSWR had 23 of the type already in use. This vehicle was intended for use in the London district, probably at Nine Elms. Its three forward gears gave it a maximum speed of 12 mph; this figure can be seen painted on the chassis, just behind the door. In anticipation of the arrival on the Southern Railway of O.V.S. Bulleid, it was fitted with 'silent chain drive,' commonplace in vehicles at that time. Although the LSWR had some Basingstoke-built Thornycroft vehicles in its fleet, the company (and subsequently the SR) continued to add Karrier vehicles to its strength. The SR was amongst the early users of the so-called 'mechanical horse', a three or four-wheeled tractor attached or detached to or from a trailer as required. The SR was using 'Karrier Cob' vehicles of this type as early as 1931. With its motorised van fleet the SR in general remained loyal to Karrier Motors or J.J. Thornycroft.

Below, right: An attempt to regain traffic from the roads was in the use of containers. This October 14 1930 photograph shows a container loaded with fruit at Covent Garden Market being off-loaded at Battersea on to a container wagon which would convey it to Dover. There it would take its place in a ship's hold as far as Calais whence it would be railborne again to Paris. The lorry, its identity obscured by the 'Southern Rly' plate on the front of the radiator, is a Karrier SK5 model. Although still heavily outnumbered by horse-drawn transport, the SR had 345 motor vehicles in service at the end of 1929. The SR also provided insulated containers for the conveyance of meat traffic. Note the suburban electric set in the background converted from former SER non bogie coaches, mainly of 1890s vintage

Left: Following an exhibition of French art treasures at Burlington House, their packing for the return journey was entrusted to a French firm, which covered all insurance risks. The paintings took ten days to pack and are here seen loaded in containers, ready to be hoisted by the Ransomes & Rapier mobile crane on to wagons, under the eagle eye of the Metropolitan Police. This operation took place at Bricklayers Arms Goods Depot on March 15 1932. The nearest trailer carries vehicle registration plate B 8528, and as this was a 1919 Lancashire registration, it is tantalising not to have a glimpse of the haulage vehicle concerned. These containers were for a Paris destination and are probably of French origin.

Above, left: The SR fleet of motorised vehicles increased in number from 316 in early 1929 to 736 in 1938. At the same time, the numbers of horse-drawn carts in service-dropped from 1,550 to 934. In addition to road vehicles a number of ancillary vehicles were in use also, for example, this battery-controlled tractor at Waterloo station, in January 1921. The driver clearly prefers his 'Silvertown Electric Truck' to having to put his back into pushing a loaded barrow.

Above, right: Also at Waterloo station, this time in October 1938, this mechanised station vacuum cleaner is clearly making a few people stop and stare. Directly behind the driver can be seen an old Bodmin & Wadebridge Railway coach. This was exhibited on the concourse, but was removed for safety during the war and is now in the care of the National Railway Museum, at York.

Right: The extent to which the SR would go to publicise its electrification programme is clearly illustrated here. A Series II Morris 10cwt van, as built between 1935 and 1939, is being used to promote the extension of the electrified lines to Bognor Regis and Littlehampton in 1938. The van is parked outside Messrs Reynolds Depositories, in Bognor Regis. Very definitely an unusual and interesting project for the railway modeller!

138

The Southern Railway, with John Elliot as its Public Relations Assistant, was very conscious of the need to advertise and promote its services. However, this essential aspect of railway work had not been overlooked by the three main pre-Grouping SR constituents, and these photographs show a display of LSWR advertising at Waterloo, in February 1916. They were photographed chiefly on the subway to the Waterloo & City tube line. Predominantly they extol the usefulness of the LSWR's then new electrification, and features a guide to the letter headcodes, P, S or V. The letters H and O were also used and the bakers of *Hovis* bread made use of this fact to illustrate five electric trains with those letters in the compartments of electric stock. Other advertisements advertise seaside resorts to be reached by the SR and even steamship routes to the Continent.

Above, left: In January 1923, this former SECR porter is pasting up a new notice headed with the words SOUTHERN RAILWAY, promoting cheap fares to the continent. The poster on the right is a reminder that the 1904-built lifting bridge known as the King's Ferry Bridge, connecting the mainland with the Isle of Sheppey had been struck on December 17 1922 by a Canadian steamship bound for Ridham Dock, leaving the island isolated. From December 27, passengers were sent via Gravesend to Port Victoria, there to embark on a boat for Sheerness and Queensborough. Two Class P 0-6-0Ts were shipped to the island on March 1, to maintain a shuttle service between the bridge and Sheerness, but normal train services were not resumed until November 1.

Above, right: 'Sunny South Sam' was a product of the fertile imagination of the SR Publicity Office, and his likeness appeared on many posters. On October 10 1933, this remarkably lifelike waxwork figure (the work of Madame Tussaud's) is on display at Brighton, as the SR's symbol of public service. 'Sam' had probably spent the summer at the London termini, hence his placard directing passengers to 'The Brighton.' The SR did much in its posters to foster the belief that it was the sunshine line. 'South for Sunshine' was another alliterative speciality of its publicity material.

WORKSHOPS

A series of photographs, regrettably without descriptions, were taken for the LSWR in June 1917 to illustrate repairs to wagon cloths, better known today as tarpaulin sheets. It seems likely that the LSWR Wagon Cloth Works remained at Nine Elms, the principal Goods Depot in London. An intriguing note in the 1921 LSWR Working Time Table Appendix states:

'Wagon sheets belonging to the Railway Companies in Britain, with the exception of those owned by the Bishop's Castle Railway and Manchester Ship Canal Company, are now available as common stock, and under no circumstances must they be passed to a foreign company (except covering loads) without the orders of the District Traffic Superintendent.

'Sheets must be removed from inward loads, and must not be allowed to remain on, or be placed in, otherwise empty wagons. When removed, they must be examined, and if found to be in good order, folded and deposited in a safe place, if possible under cover, and in no case must a sheet be allowed to remain on the ground in a position where it might prove to an obstruction to staff in execution of their duties.

'In the event of a sheet being found defective, it should be forwarded to the Storekeeper, Nine Elms, without delay. It

Above: In June 1917, four women are busy in the LSWR Wagon Cloth Works, apparently patching old wagon cloths for further use. The sheets were hung up first on the wall behind, where holes were circled in chalk, ready for patching.

should be invoiced to that station, with the remark 'For Repairs' and an entry of the sheet with the painted number should be made on the ticking-off notes.'

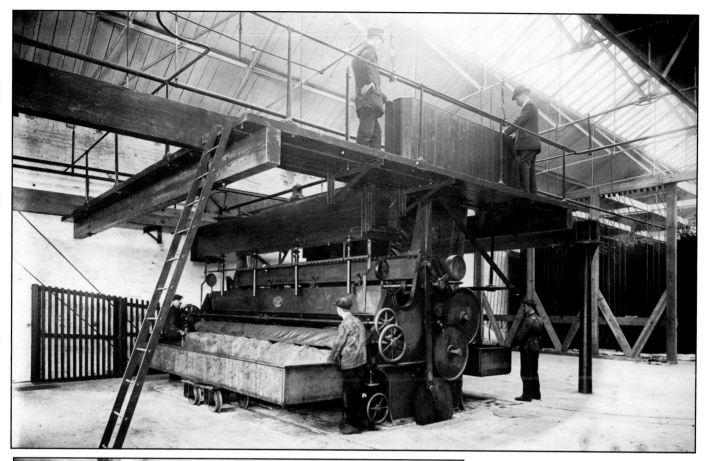

Above: Although no caption survives for this June 1917 view, it seems likely that this machine was used for applying water-proofer to the repaired or new wagon cloths, which were then hung to dry on the tall-racks in the background.

Left: This 1913 picture of a party being shown round Southampton Docks shows that wagon cloths were not confined to rail wagons, but also horse-drawn wagons.

anything liable to be ignited by sparks from the engine or liable to damage from damp, such as cement. The notice is not explicit on the subject of manure, other than stating:

'Manure and horse refuse traffic via Beckenham: This route must be used as little as possible for transferring trucks containing this traffic, but when necessary, care must be taken to see it is despatched by such trains as will make a quick connection, so that it is not held at Beckenham for more than two hours.'

In fact such traffic was sheeted in transit, as was hay, straw and the like. On the LBSCR, defective truck sheets were locked in a covered wagon and despatched to New-haven Town for repair.

The SECR 1922 Appendix is even more explicit stating that Sheets must not be provided for the under-mentioned traffic:

Agricultural implements; Bones (whether loose or in bags), Hoofs and Horns; Bottles (in bags, unless packed in straw involving risk of a fire); Coal tar pitch (in blocks); Deals; Battens; Boards; Firewood; Granite dust; Limestone (in bulk); Pyrites (not burnt); Salt (in owners wagons); Scrap iron and steel; Slag (in bulk); Tallow; Zinc concentrates.

It is less helpful otherwise, apart from stating that saltpetre bags, wet salted hides and cast iron borings should be sheeted. Clearly, the sheeting rule applied equally to

Right: A February 1918 view of the then comparatively new Foundry at Eastleigh Works. The overhead travelling crane carried the vat from which molten metal was poured during the casting process.

RAILWAYMEN AT WORK

Above: This interesting experiment in automatic coupling took place at the former LBSCR Carriage & Wagon Works, at Lancing, on March 28 1924. Engineers from railways in Britain and overseas attended the demonstration. The coupling was the invention of a South African, the late W.G. Boonzaier. It became known as the Gearlock-Reynard coupling. The 'Gearlock' was a vertical plane central buffer coupling for automatically coupling goods wagons, while the 'Reynard' was an accessory for automatically coupling up brakes, steam pipes, and electric connections. It was never adopted. The coupling was designed to give immunity from accident to those engaged in shunting operations. This view reveals that whilst automatic in operation, the jaws of the coupling had to be opened manually from the trackside, by pulling the chain. The late Mr Boonzaier had developed this coupling from that shown at Clapham Junction in 1921 and it was reported that it worked equally well on straight and curved track and weighed 6cwt, compared with the 12cwt of hook and link couplings.

Above: During LSWR days at Nine Elms yard, a uniformed shunter gives a demonstration of handsignals, as used to indicate required movements to the drivers of yard locomotives

Left: The original Topical Press Agency caption to this June 8 1935 picture is headed: "The Whitsun Holiday Rush," although a rush is hardly evident in this scene! The child is said to be enquiring:"Please, where is the sunshine?" Note the poster advertising the SR's 'Bournemouth Belle' service, featuring a stylised 'Lord Nelson' 4-6-0. Posters of this type now bring large sums at auctions of railway memorabilia.

Above: A handshake from the Wimbledon Stationmaster for a Foreman about to retire from the Company's service. On the left is a typical SR concrete station nameboard manufactured at the SR's Exmouth Junction Concrete Works.

Left: Produced by the SR's own Publicity Office and distributed for free use by newspapers and magazines, this picture illustrates the extent to which the company promoted not only its passenger services, but also new innovations. The date is May 9 1946 and the picture was taken to depict new high-pressure cleaning machines; the SR announced that the same job performed manually would take five times as long. The locomotive is Maunsell 'U' class 2-6-0 No. 1616.